AUSTRALIA
A Picture Book to Remember Her by

CRESCENT BOOKS
NEW YORK

Text by Rupert O. Matthews
CLB 1082
© 1987 Illustrations and text: Colour Library Books Ltd.,
   Guildford, Surrey, England.
Text filmsetting by Acesetters Ltd., Richmond, Surrey, England.
All rights reserved.
Printed and bound in Barcelona, Spain by Cronion, S.A.
1987 edition published by Crescent Books, distributed by Crown Publishers, Inc.
ISBN 0 517 52021 7
h g f e d c b a

It does rain in Australia, but that is not the image which most people have of the continent. As far as most people are concerned it is a land of sunshine, cloudless skies and swimming temperatures. To a large extent it is, of course, true that Australia is a land of sunshine and heat, but that is not the whole story. In a land as large as this it is inevitable that there will be great variatioms in climate, for weather is unstable. Air masses move in from south, north and east, jostling for position over the country.

In Darwin, a city which spends the majority of the year basking beneath rainless skies, comes a forceful reminder that Australia is not all clear skies. For three months of the year the monsoons sweep across the city, bringing high temperatures and torrential rains. While temperatures regularly top the 100 degree Fahrenheit mark, the clouds dump all but an inch of the five feet of rain which Darwin receives each year. It is not a good time to visit the capital of the Northern Territory unless you enjoy being drenched by lukewarm rain. Elsewhere, the seasons bring equally distinctive changes. In Brisbane, for example, the three summer months bring blankets of cloud and a stifling humidity which makes it as uncomfortable as it is idyllic during the rest of the year. The beaches of the Gold and Sunshine Coasts are most crowded with sun-bronzed bodies during the finer months of the year, when they bask in a climate equalled by nowhere else and the envy of many.

The most confused weather of all must be that of Melbourne. It is a good deal further south than other mainland capitals and so has, on the whole, cooler weather. Summer days only rarely top the 100 degree mark and ice has even been known to form in the depths of winter. It is not this, however, that makes Melbourne's weather so notable. The position of the city, with the proximity of the Australian Alps and two great oceans, results in a number of influences competing for control of the weather. This can result in clear, sunny skies being swept away by rain-laden air masses, which in turn vanish to be replaced by howling winds. And all this in the space of a single day.

It is not only the cities which make up Australia, however, and by far the greatest stretch of the country lies far beyond their confines. Here, in the open reaches of countryside, the landscape is determined as much by the climate as by anything else. Along the eastern coast of the continent, between the mountains and the ocean, is a strip of land ranging from the tropical to the temperate. In the north rich, tropical vegetation holds sway, while in the far south the vegetation is quite different. The whole seaboard, however, shares many characteristics. Here rainfall is spread throughout the year, without the dramatic monsoons of Darwin. Likewise the temperature range is moderate, without the excesses noted elsewhere. The two features combine to produce a climate which aids the fertility of the land. A rich cloak of green covers the eastern slopes of the mountains and the coastal plain. It is here that much of Australia's agriculture is carried on, along the productive lands which first attracted European settlers.

By the time the easterly winds have crossed the mountains they have shed most of the rain, and this profoundly affects the landscape. The rolling countryside is covered by vast stretches of grassland where sheep, cattle and kangaroos graze beneath cloudless skies. Further to the west the land becomes progressivley drier until the grass gives way to scrubland, and eventually desert. Though few people live in the dry interior, it covers the vast majority of the land and has come to typify the nation abroad. Endless horizons of treeless plains and shattered outlines of rock-strewn hills make up the heart of the continent. Stretching on across the Gibson, Canning and Great Sandy Deserts, the barren lands drop into the Indian Ocean. It is only in the far southwest, where the prevailing winds sweep in from the west laden with moisture, that the desert is relieved. Here the land bursts forth in a welter of greenery and vivid colours. Around Perth the land is awash with wildflowers which have evolved in isolation from the rest of the world.

Huge and varied, this land is a product of its climatic range, and whilst much of the continent may be parched, it certainly does rain in Australia.

The Erskine Falls in the Otway Ranges, near Lorne, Victoria.

Northern Queensland has some of the world's most beautiful beaches, including those near Cairns (left and top), Port Douglas (above) and on Green Island (facing page) on the Great Barrier Reef.

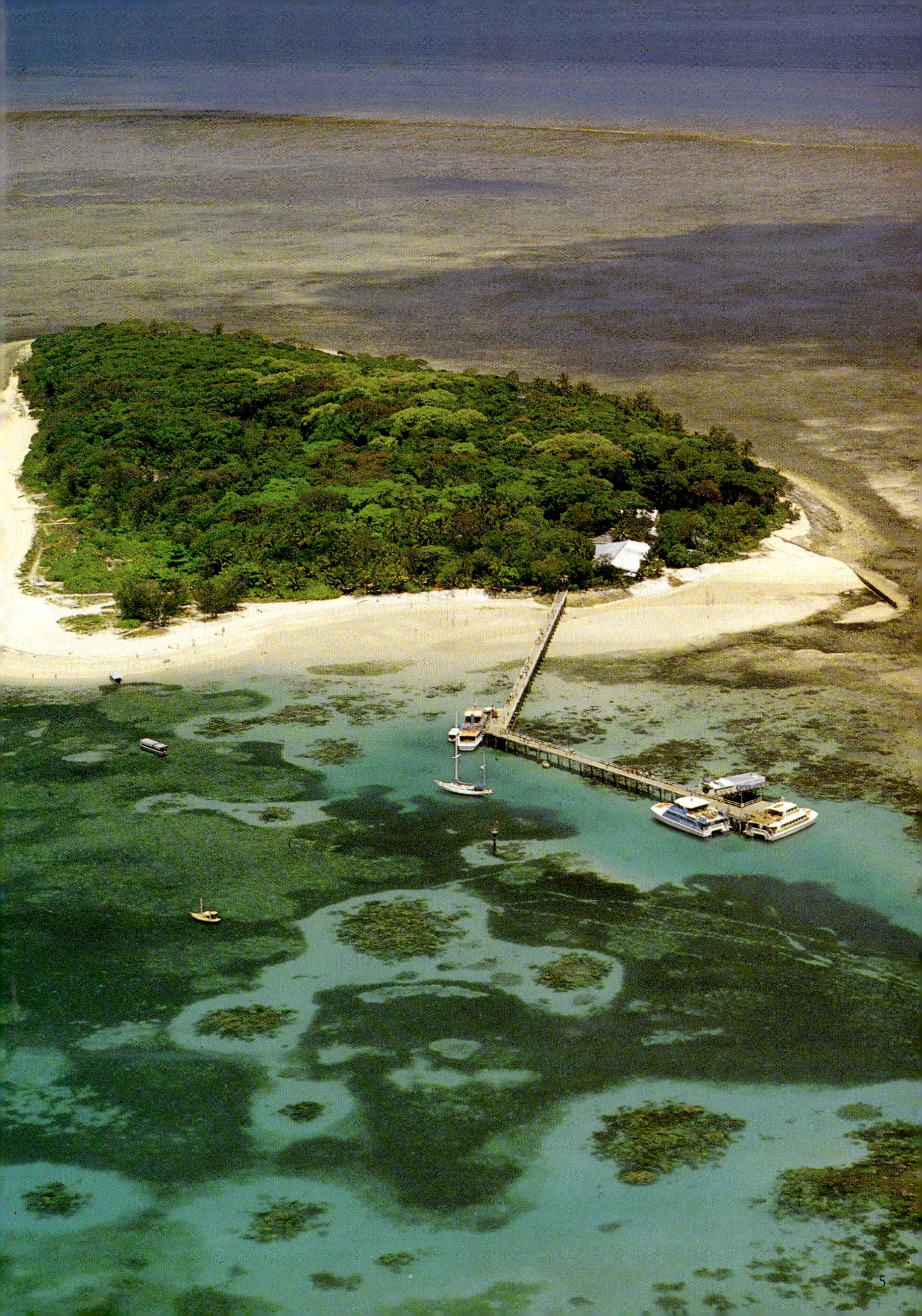

Founded in 1876, Cairns (top and facing page, top) soon became a centre for sugar cane growing (facing page, bottom) which is still a source of prosperity, along with bananas (above). Left: the 'Singing Ship' memorial to Captain Cook, near Yeppoon.

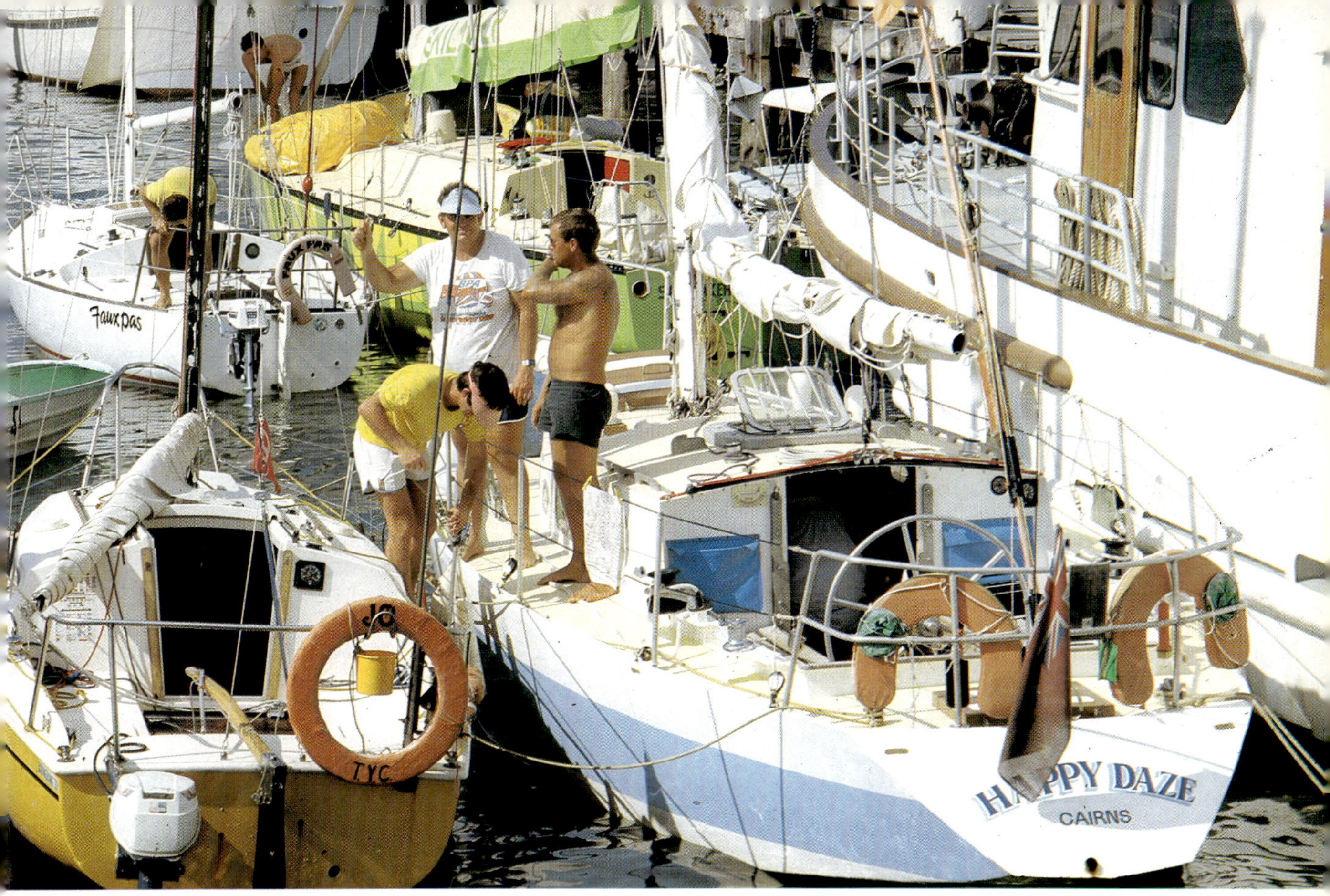
Faux pas
T.Y.C.
HAPPY DAZE
CAIRNS

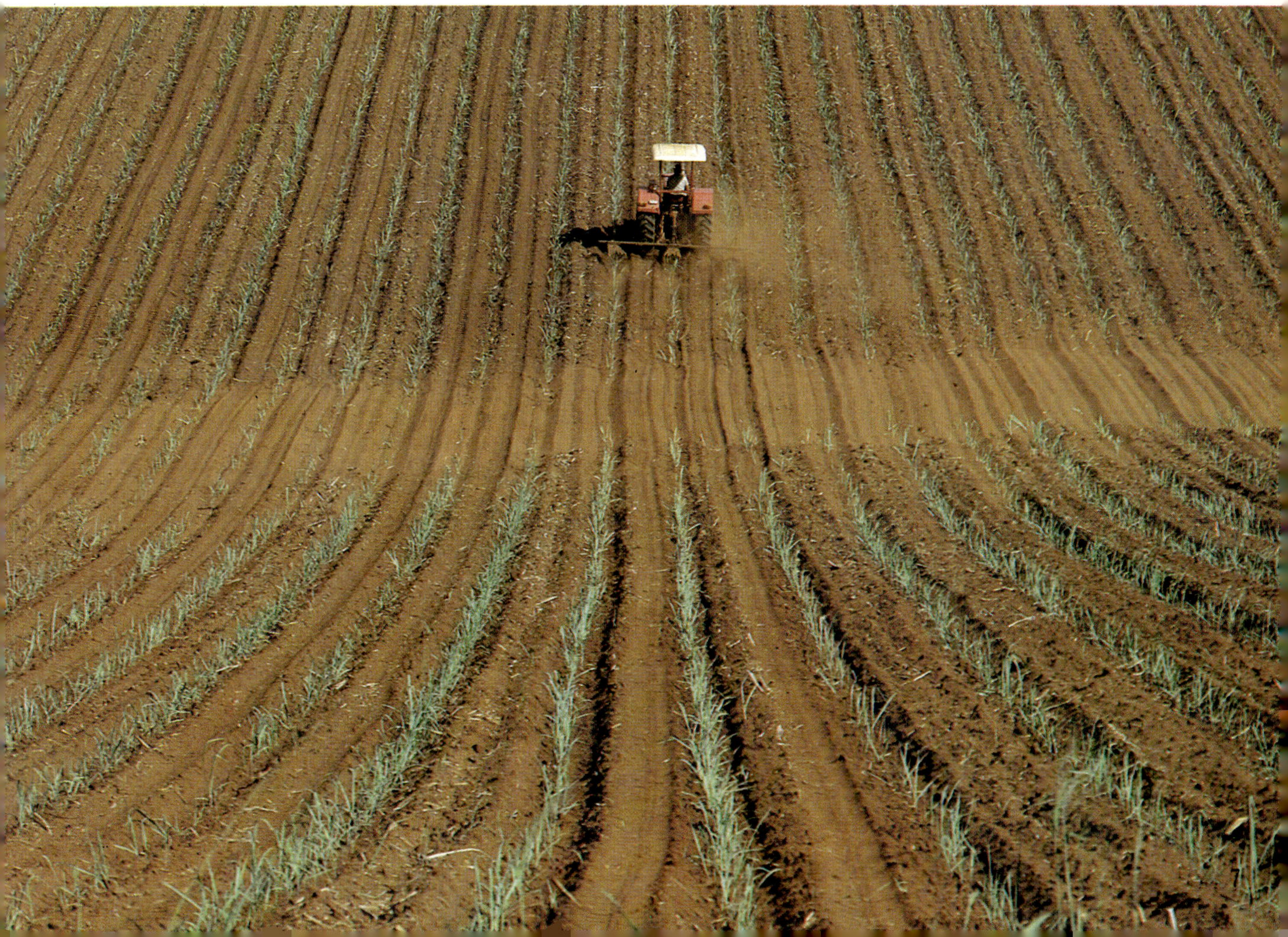

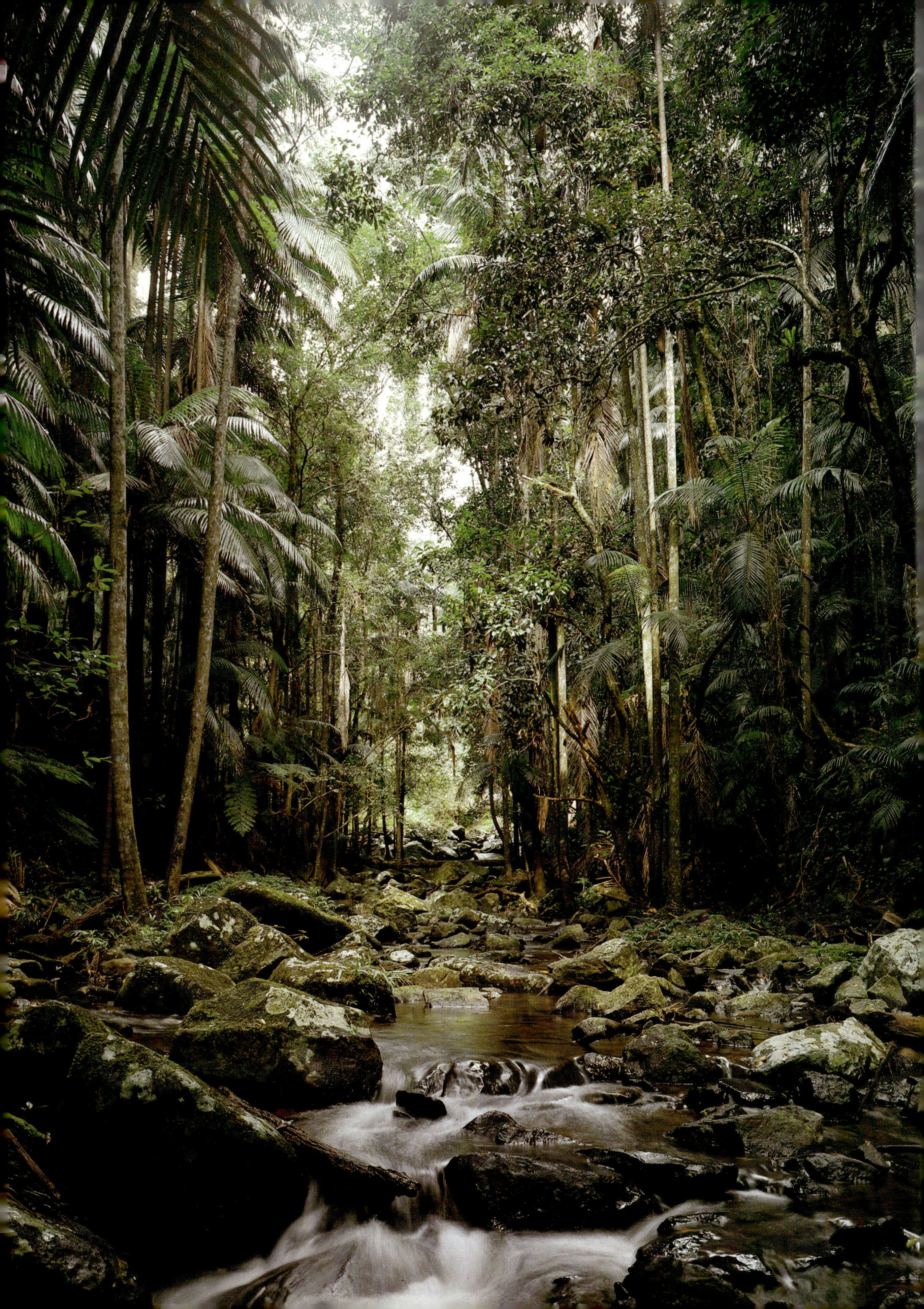

The forests and hills of southern Queensland contain some of the most atmospheric beauty in Australia. Cedar Creek (facing page) and Curtis Falls (left) provide cool havens amid the forest. Carnarvon Gorge contains the Moss Garden (top) and fascinating examples of Aboriginal art (above).

Brisbane, the capital of Queensland, was the first successful European settlement in sub-tropical conditions and boomed with the state's growth in agriculture and pastoralism. King George Square contains both the City Hall (facing page) and the Methodist Church (left). Above: the Queensland Club and (top) Captain Cook Bridge.

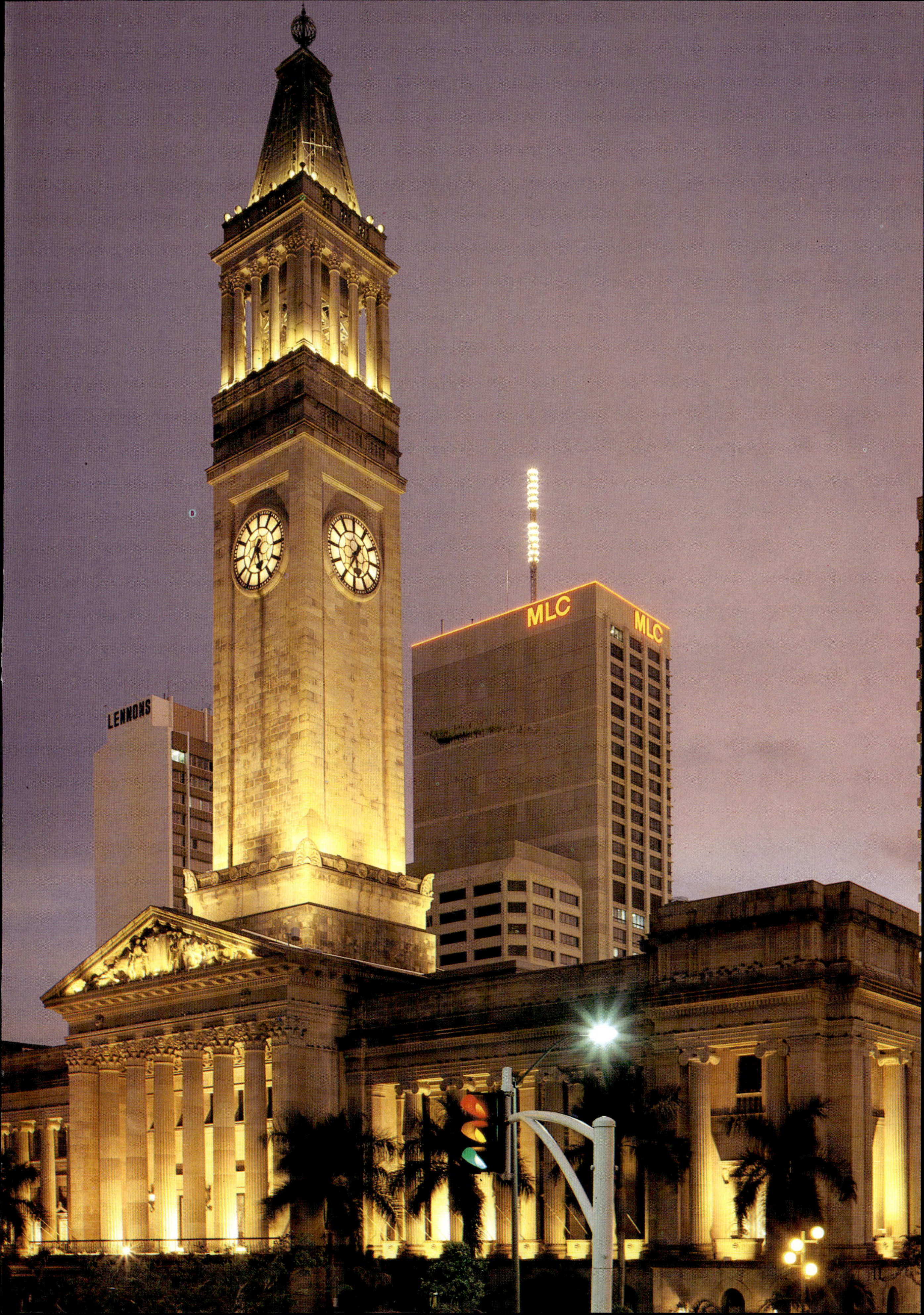
LENNONS
MLC
MLC

Above and top: ultra-modern Surfers Paradise came into being following the building booms of the 1950s and 60s. Today, it is one of the most popular holiday resorts in Australia. City of the Gold Coast (left and facing page), the name given to the ribbon of land between Southport and Coolangatta, also enjoys continued popularity.

13

Coffs Harbour (above) is an important port in northern New South Wales. Top: Stanwell Park, south of Sydney. Facing page: the Ellenborough Falls, north of Wingham, on the Bulga Plateau.

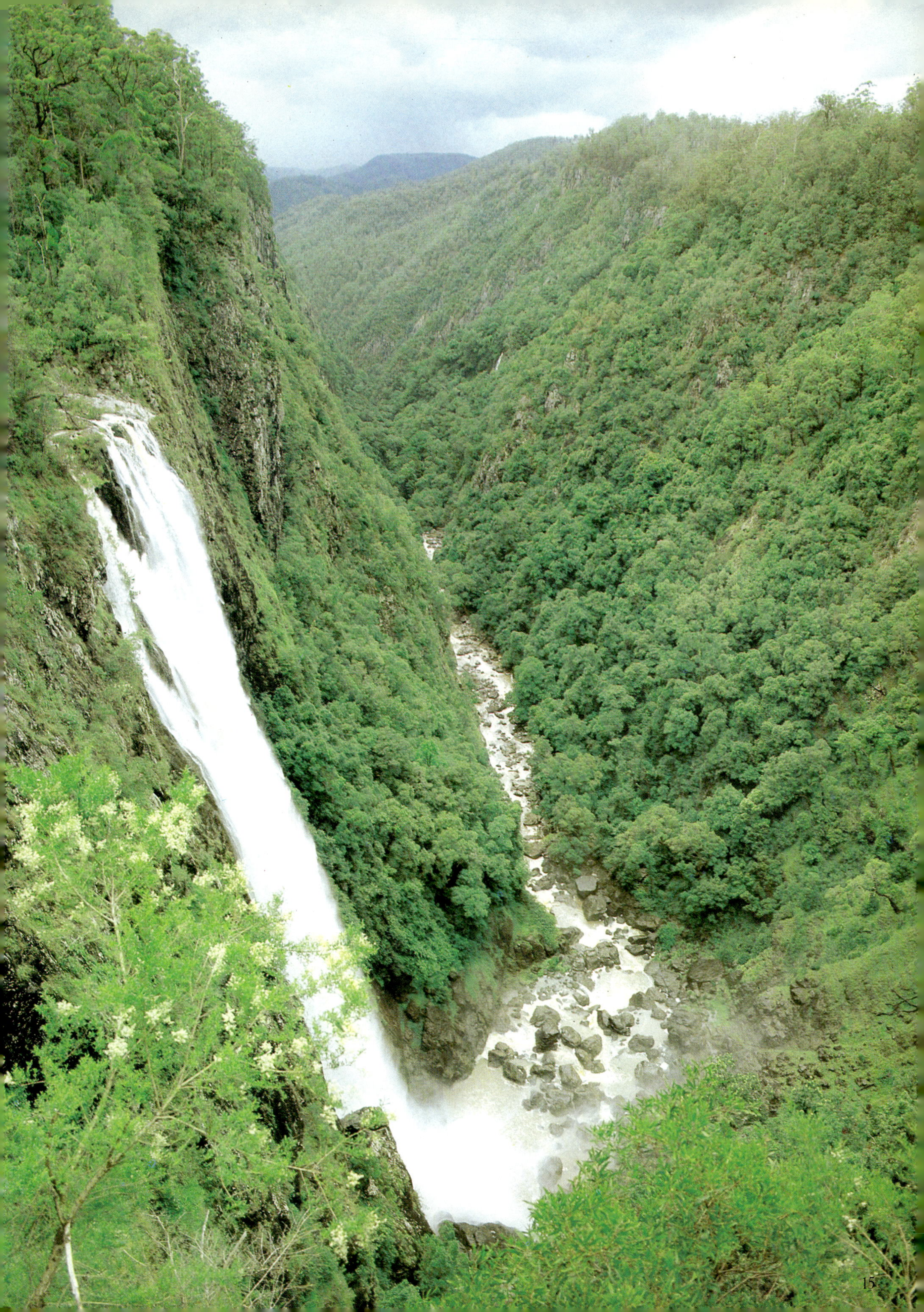

Sydney's natural setting is complemented by its many man-made attractions, which include the Harbour Bridge (facing page top) and the Opera House (facing page bottom). The restored Rocks area (top), as well as colourful Chinatown (above) are always popular, while the Strand Arcade (left) offers modern shopping in elegant Victorian surroundings.

17

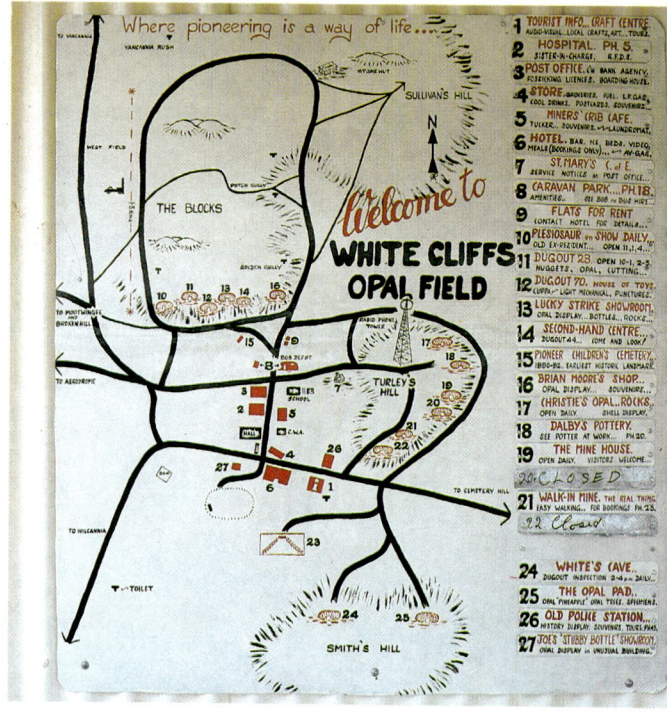

Top: Bronte Beach, near Sydney. Left: Blue Lagoon, inland from Sydney. Above: a map of the outback town of White Cliffs. Facing page: Wentworth Falls, in the Blue Mountains.

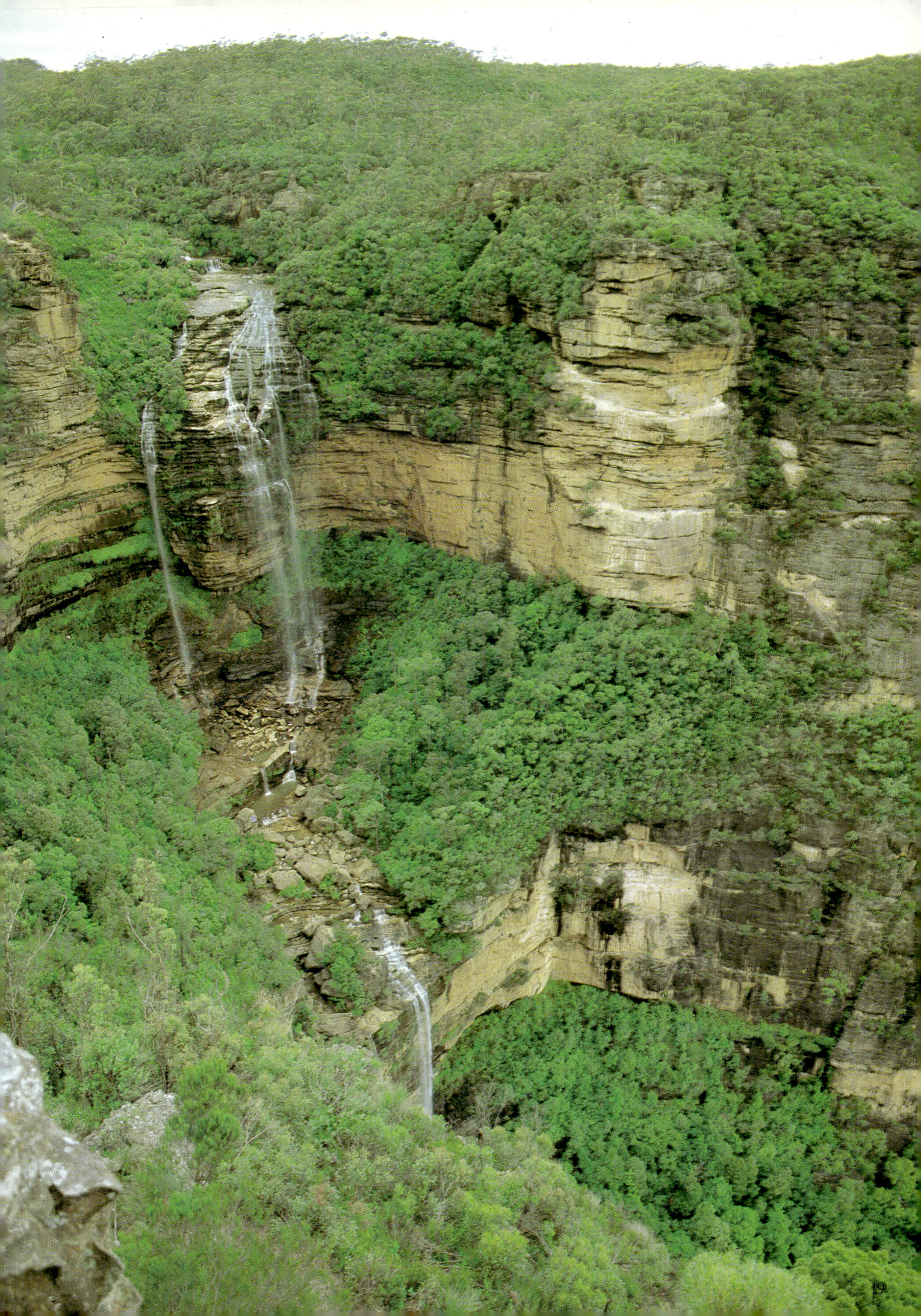

In 1913 work began on a new capital for Australia which was intended, by its designer Walter Burley Griffin, to be 'like no other city in the world'. At its heart lies Lake Burley Griffin with its distinctive Captain Cook Memorial (facing page) and the Carillon (left), which stands on an island in the lake. Above: Number 2 Courtroom in the High Court of Australia. Top: Parliament House and Anzac Parade.

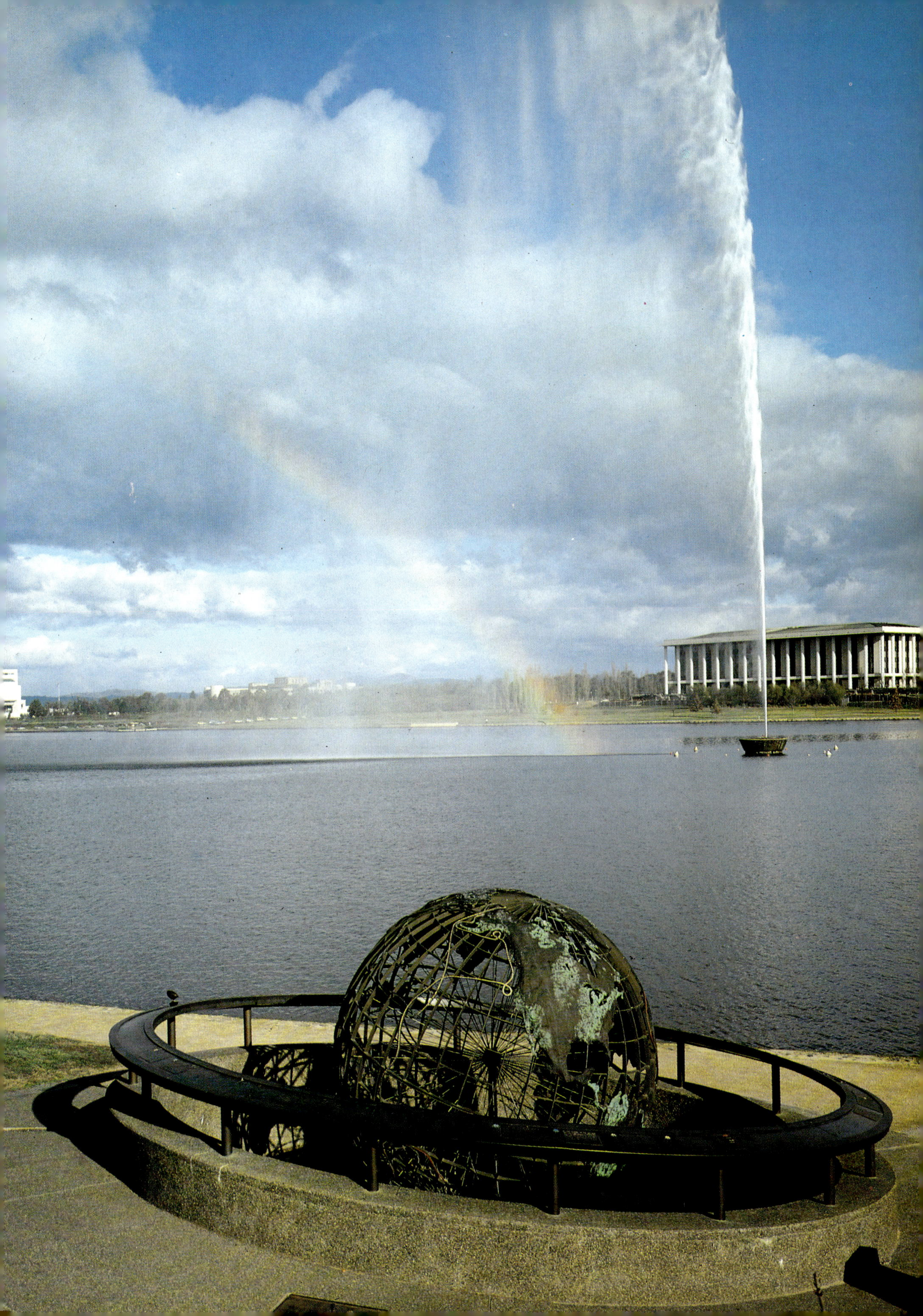

These pages: from central Canberra (above and top) to its outlying areas, the clean, spare lines of modern architecture grace a variety of buildings, from important cultural institutions such as the Australian National Gallery (top left), to more functional establishments like the Bus Station (left). Facing page: (top) the Byzantine-style Australian War Memorial and (bottom) the vacation snowfields of the Perisher Valley.

23

Southeastern New South Wales contains some of the most varied scenery in the state. Kosciusko National Park, with Charlottes Pass (top), is the largest park in the state, covering some 620,000 hectares of hills, grasslands and forests. Above: hang-gliding at Stanwell Park. Right: the marina at Wollongong. Facing page: (top) the Clyde River Bridge at Batemans Bay and (bottom) Port Kembla, part of the thriving industrial centre of Greater Wollongong.

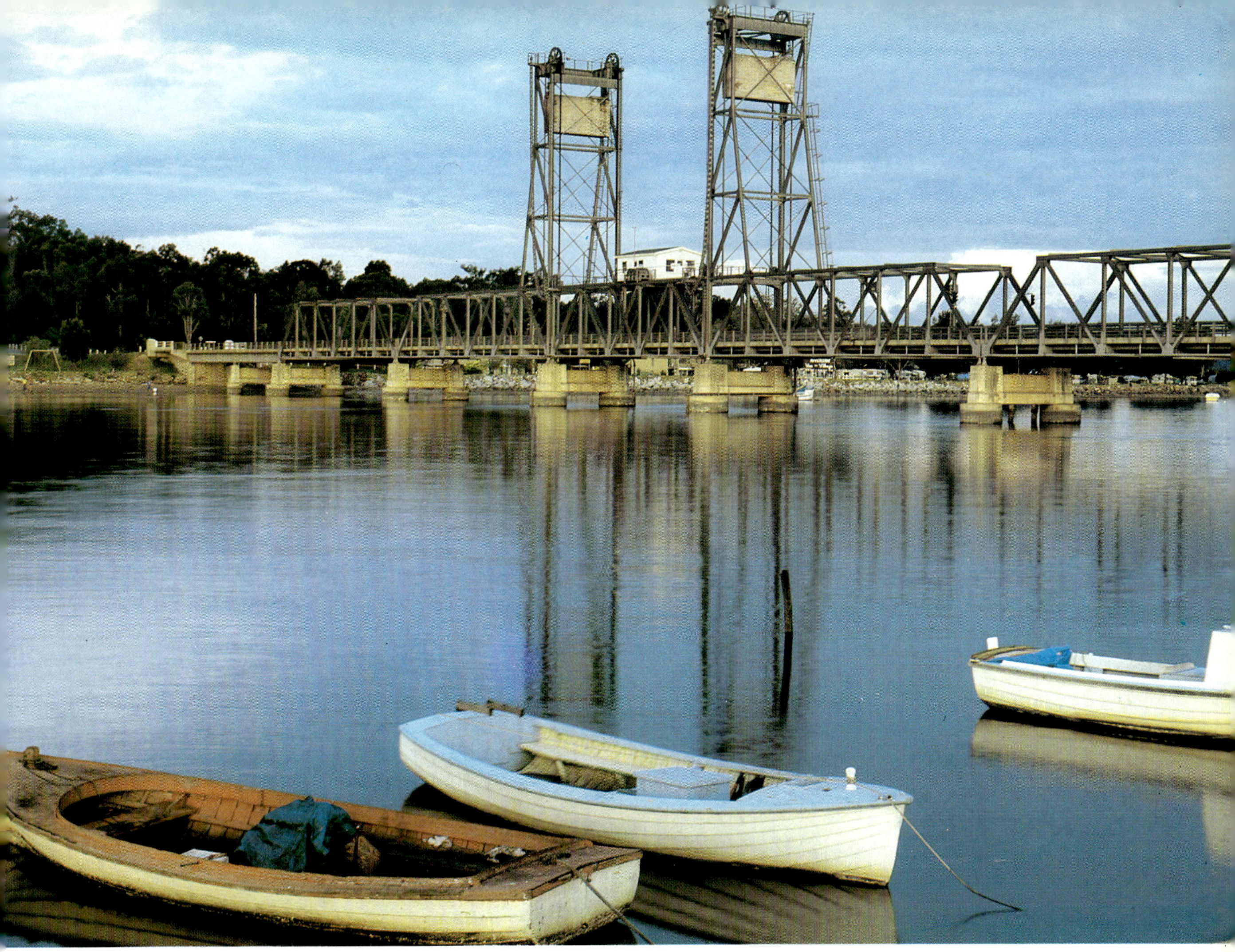

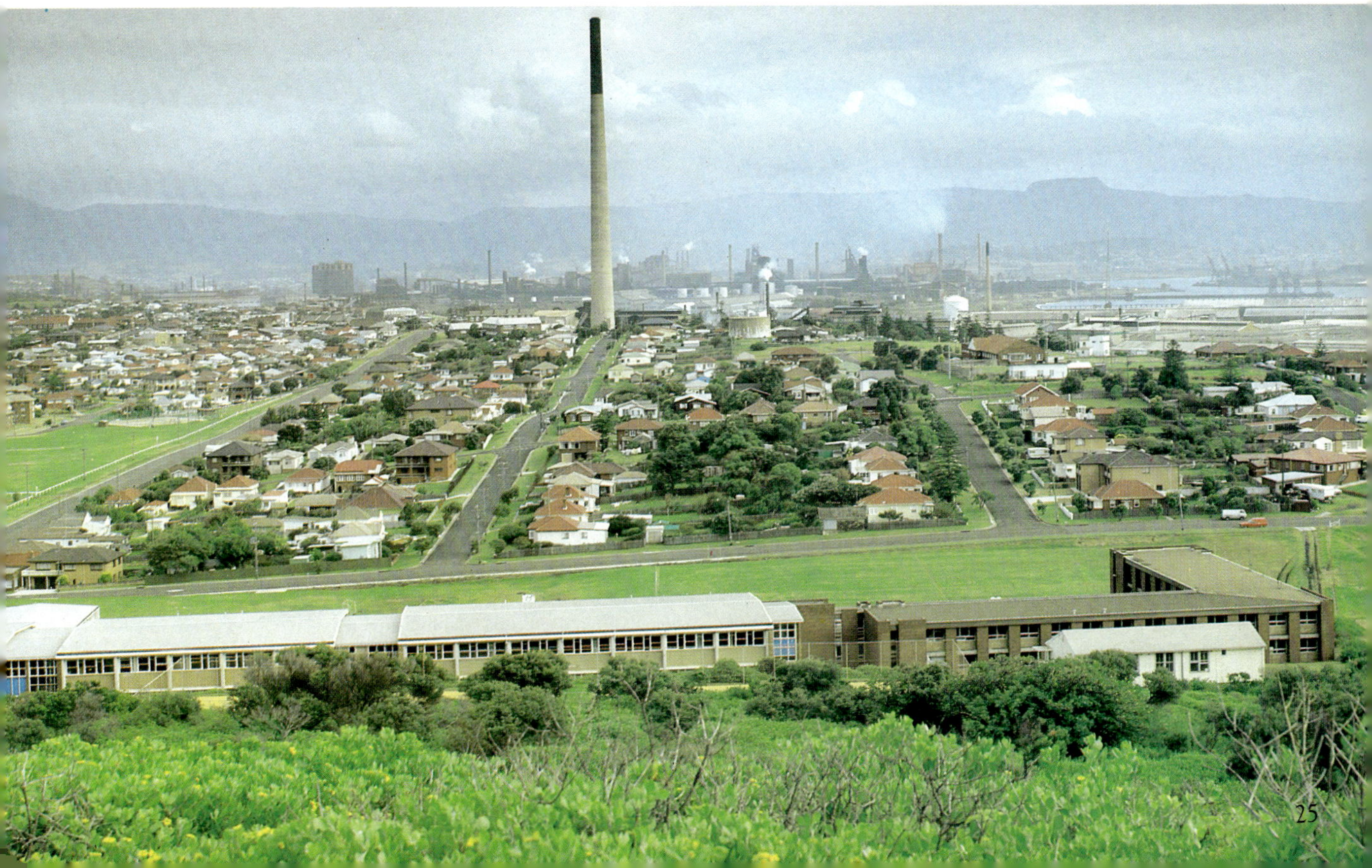

These pages: Victoria. Top: a suspension bridge across a leafy gorge near Yarram in Gippsland. Above: a tranquil scene in Sorrento, near the mouth of Port Phillip Bay. Facing page: (top) sunset at Squeaky Beach in Wilsons Promontory National Park and (bottom) Pyramid Rock which, like Bourne Creek (left), is on Phillip Island.

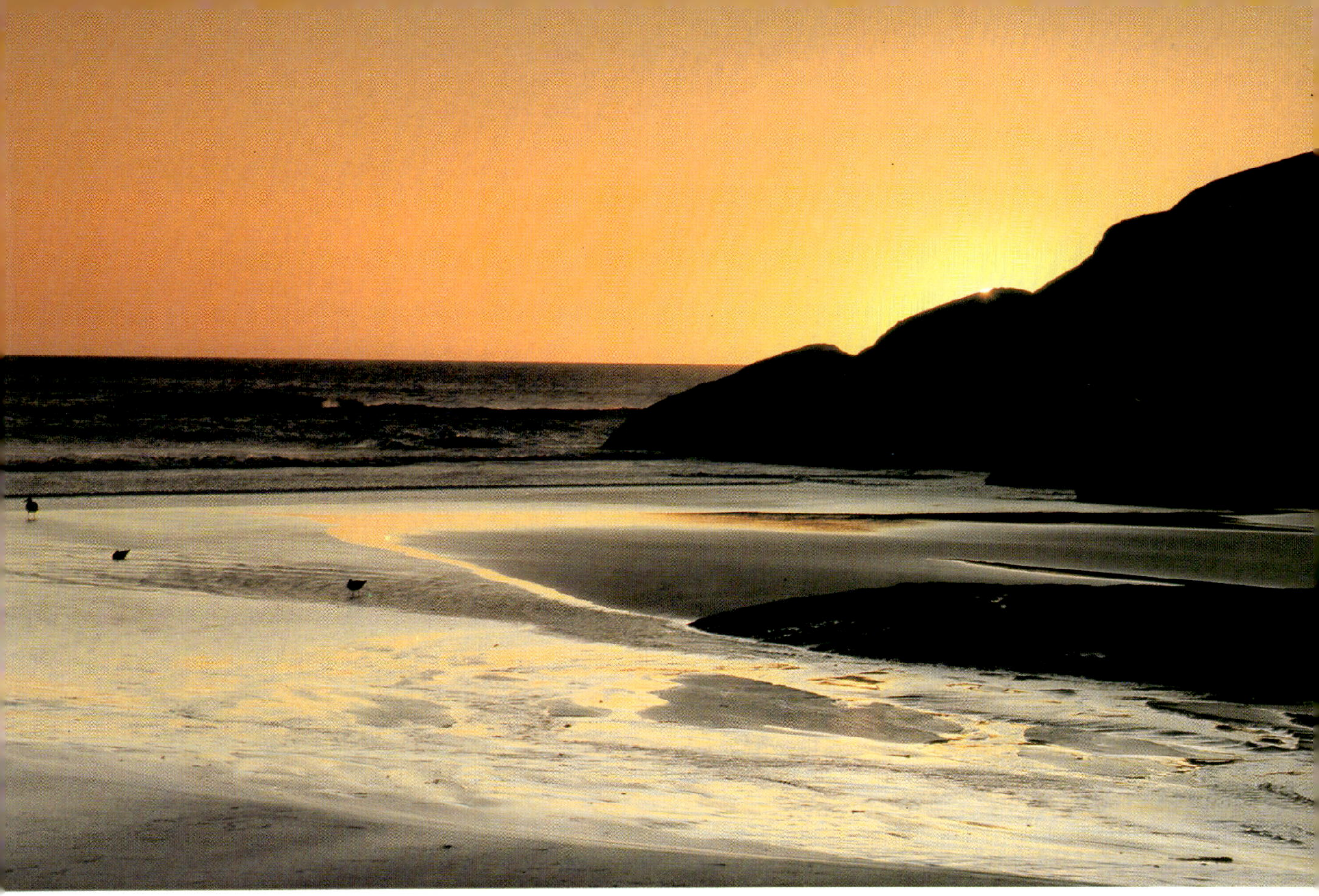

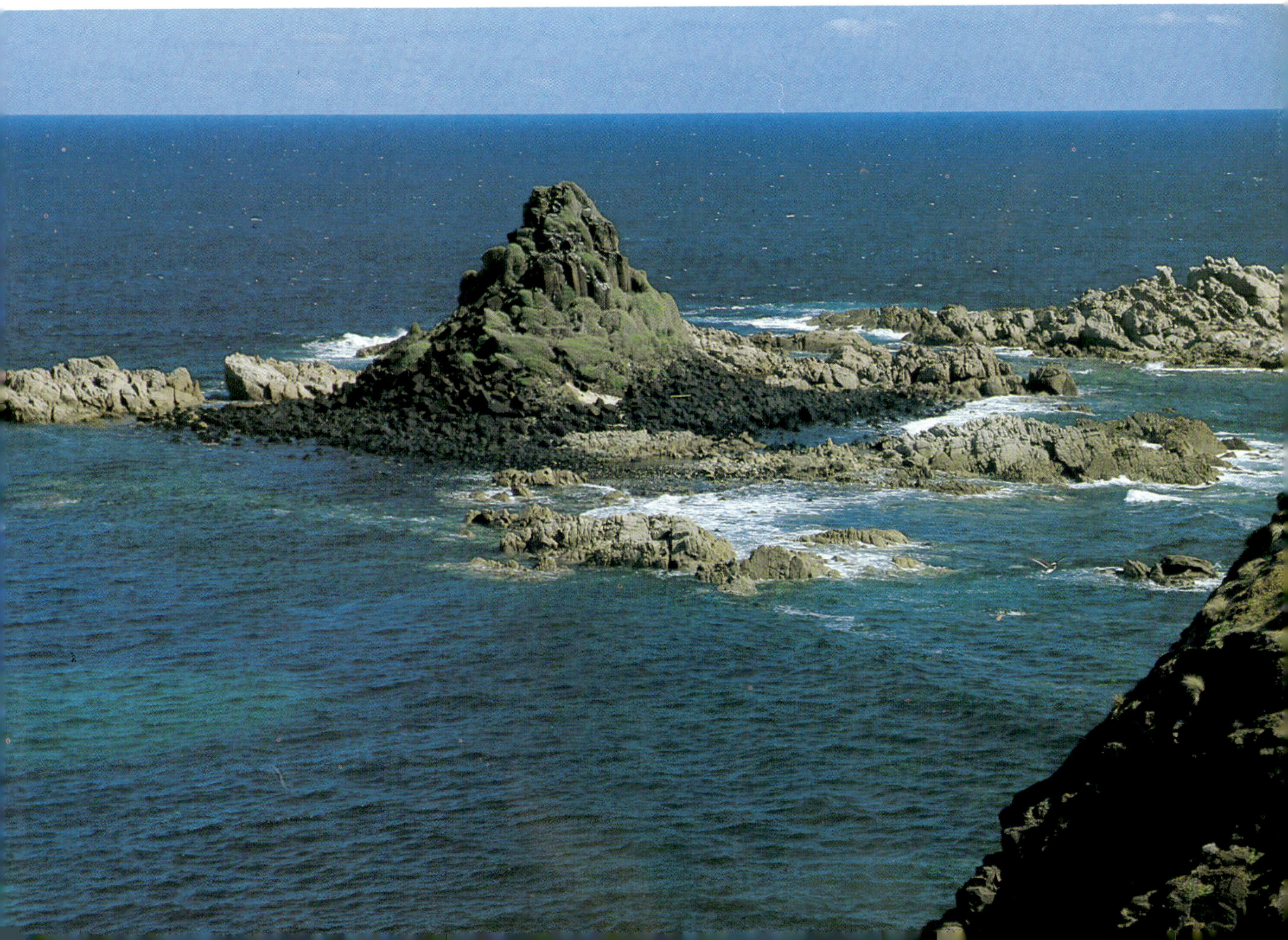

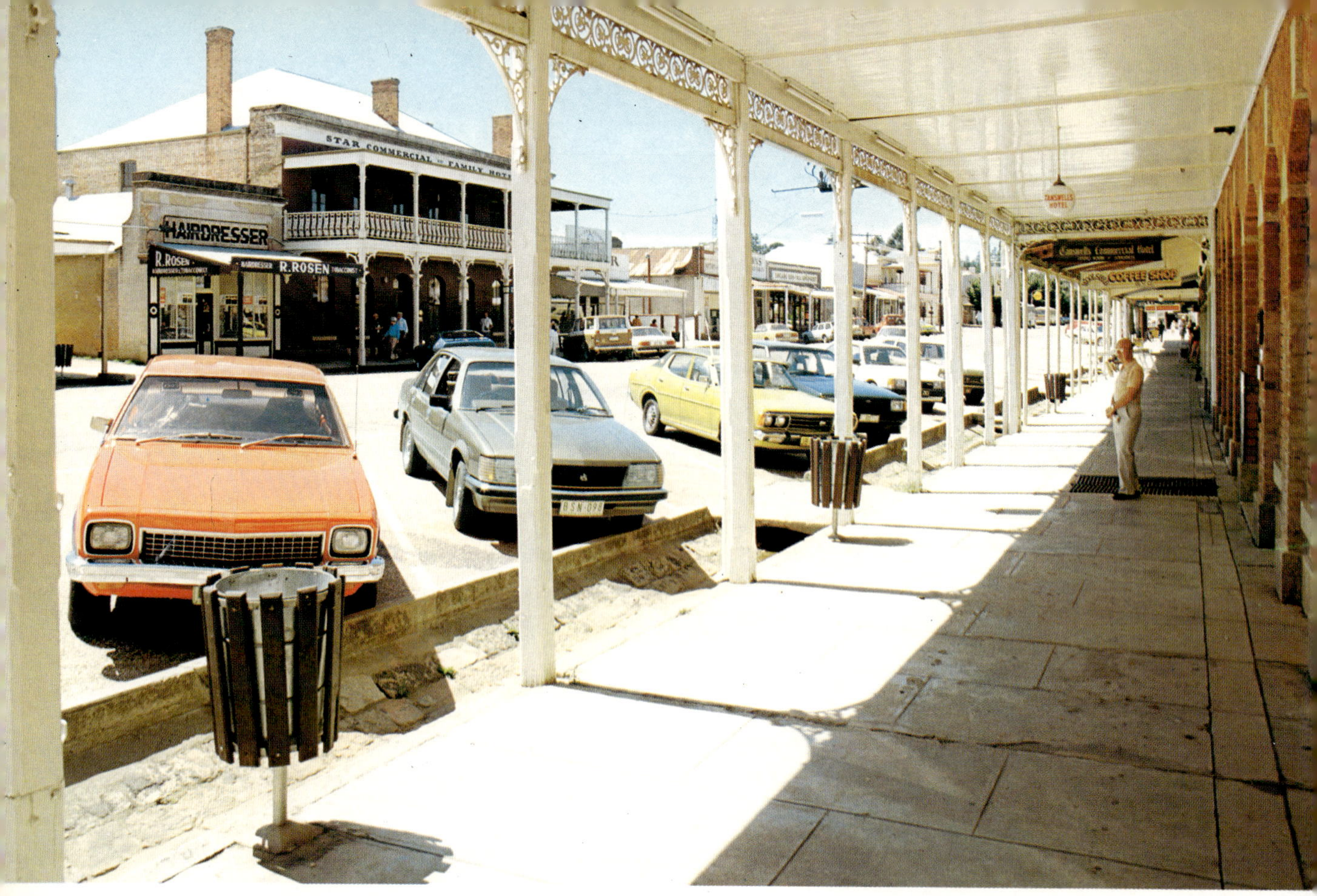

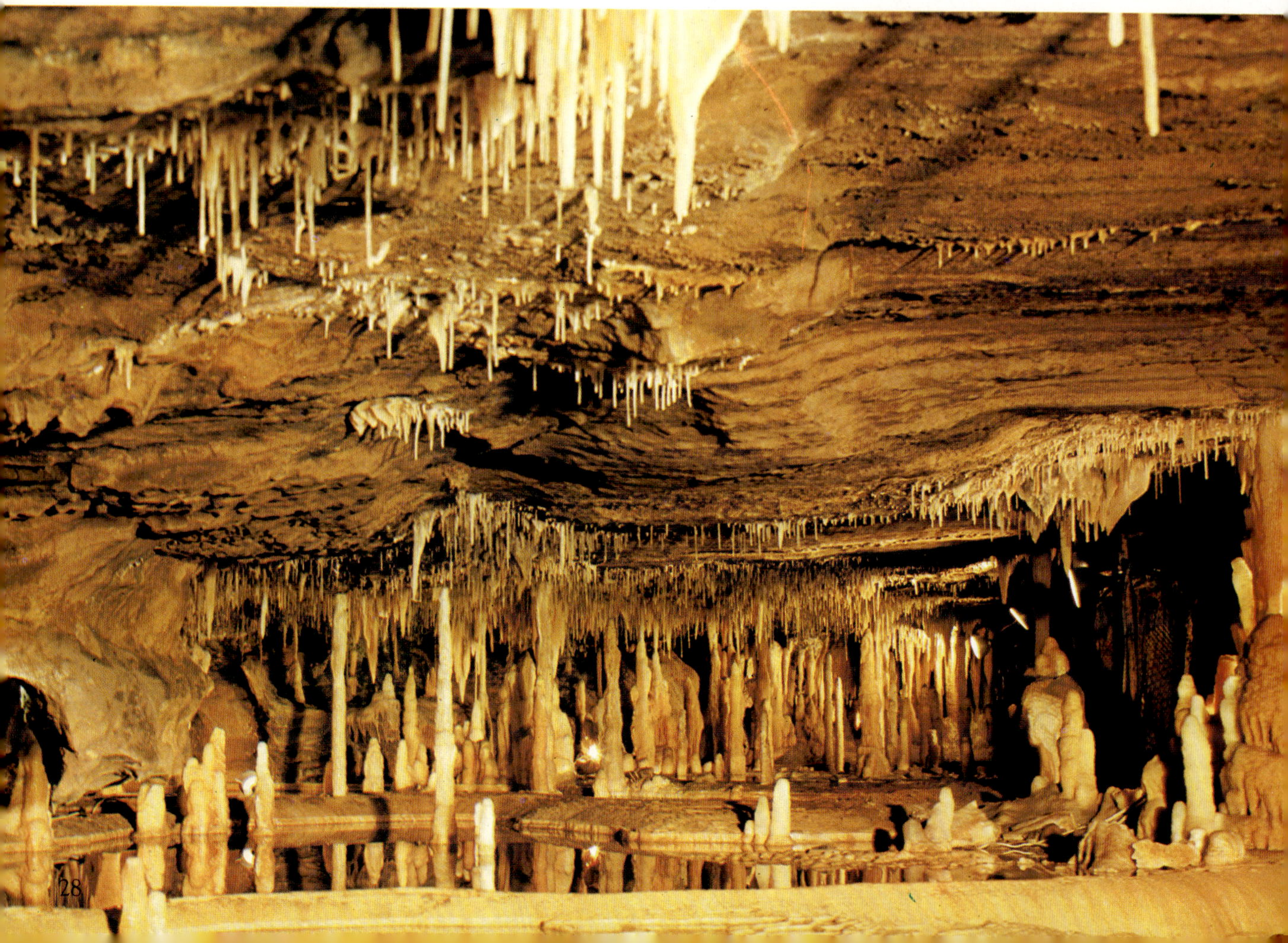

Above: Kates Cottage, the reconstructed home of Ned Kelly, near Glenrowan. Right: Bairnsdale, (top) sunset near Sale, and (facing page, bottom) Royal Cave, near Buchan, all in Gippsland.
Facing page top: the historic town of Beechworth.

Melbourne is the elegant city of Australia. It is now the capital of the 'Garden State' of Victoria, but was once the capital of the nation and maintains the atmosphere of a bustling metropolis. The city has come a long way since 1835, when pioneers led by John Batman established a settlement on the site, and now has many fine and imposing buildings such as the Cathedral of Saint Patrick (left), Flinders Street Station (below), Bourke Street Mall (bottom), the Exhibition Buildings (facing page, top), and the ultra-modern Victorian Arts Centre (facing page, bottom).

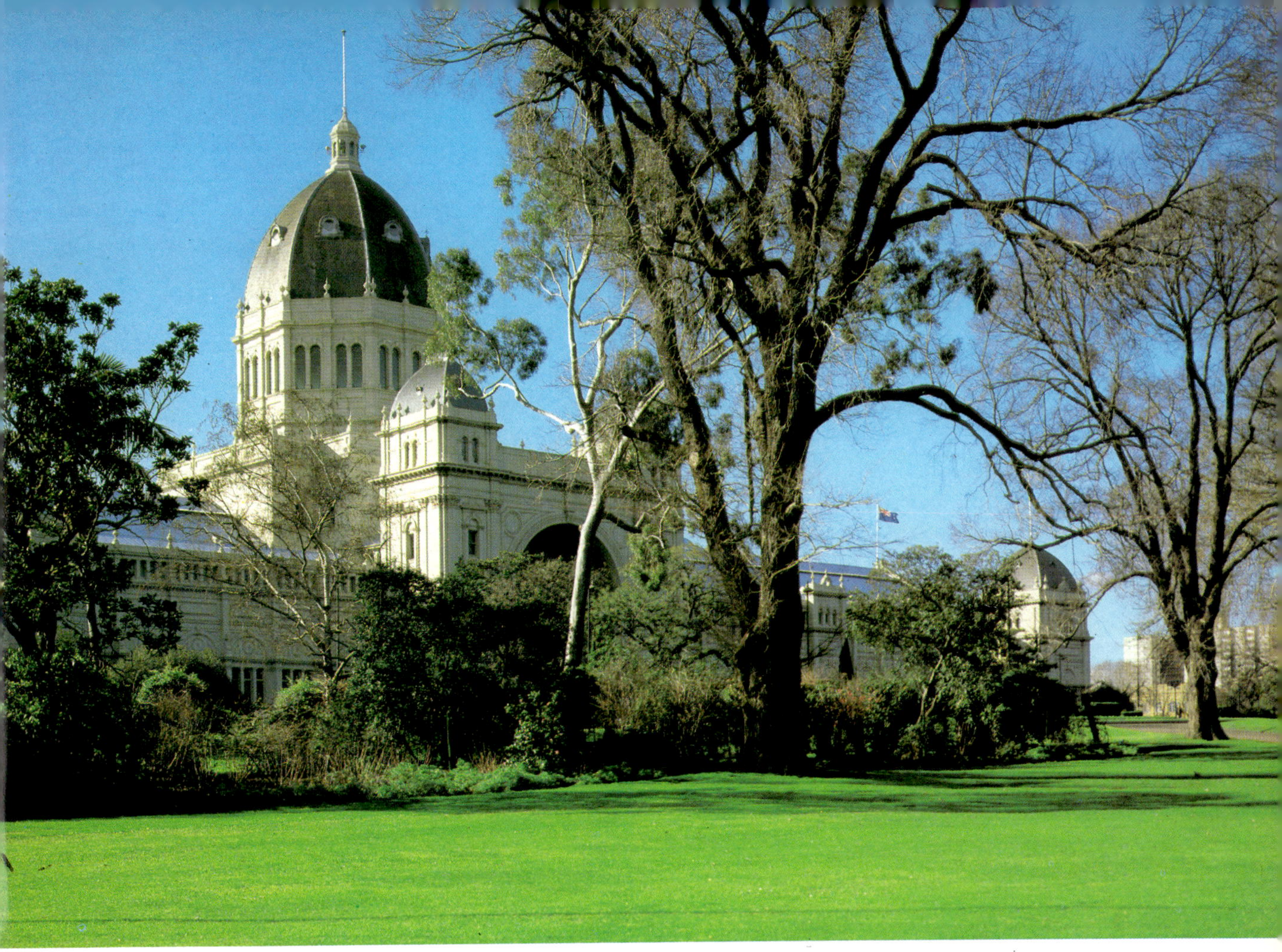

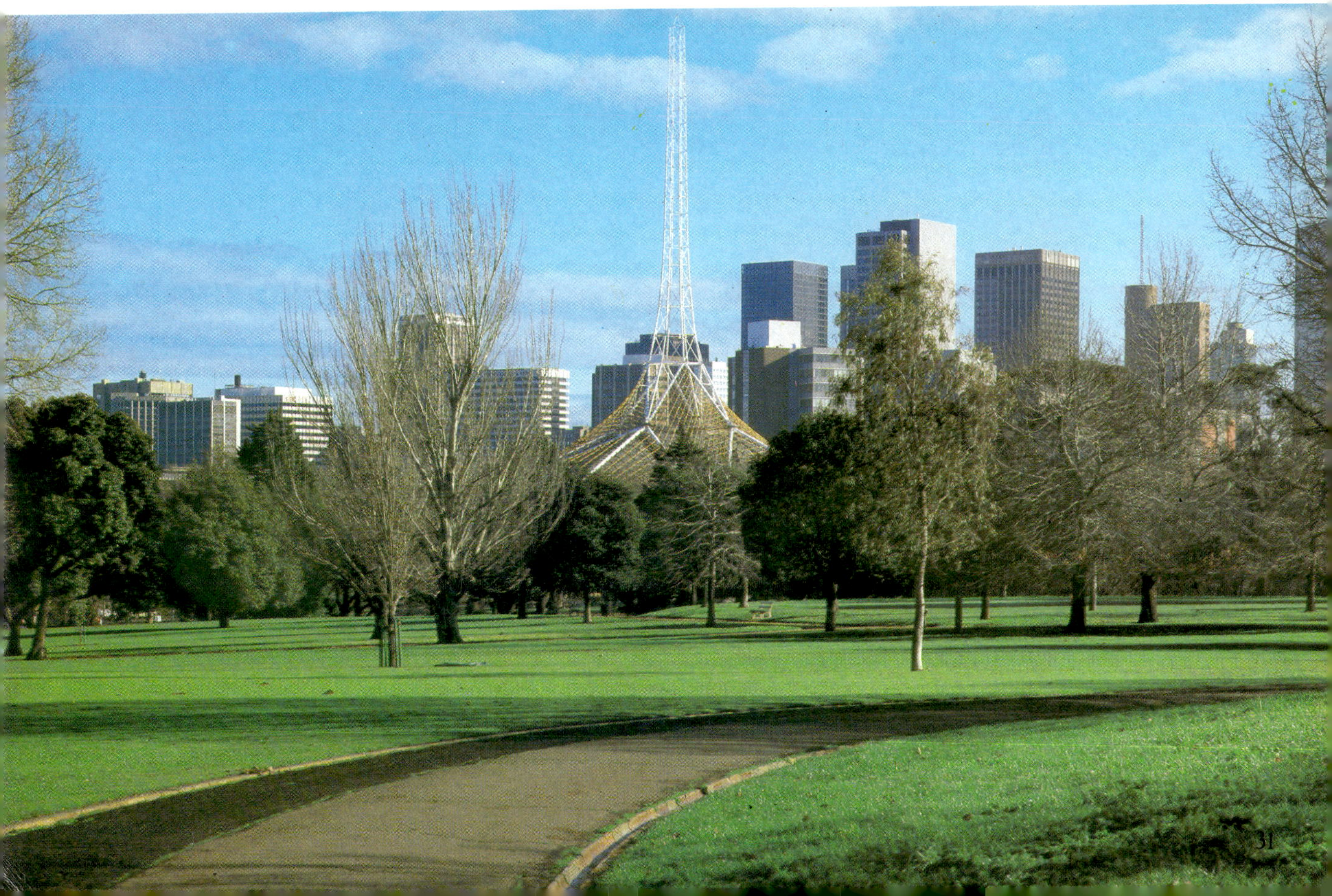

TRAM TOUR
BENDIGO'S
VINTAGE 'TALKING' TRAM
TOUR.
LEAVES THIS POINT
TIME TABLE
BENDIGO TRAMWAYS
Nº 30
LITTER

The Swan Hill Pioneer Settlement (right) preserves many buildings and machines from the early days of settlement in Victoria. Top: paddleships at Echuca remind the visitor of the importance of the town as a river port in the latter half of last century. Sovereign Hill (above), a popular tourist attraction in Ballarat, faithfully recreates the buildings and atmosphere of the gold rush days. Facing page: a tram in Pall Mall, Bendigo.

33

Top: Hamilton, in western Victoria. Remaining pictures: Mildura, which is the centre of one of Australia's first irrigated areas and has become the hub of a wine producing region, with many vineyards (above) in the vicinity. Left: a fountain on Deakin Street (facing page, top), and (bottom) the bar, allegedly the world's longest, in Mildura's Workingman's Club.

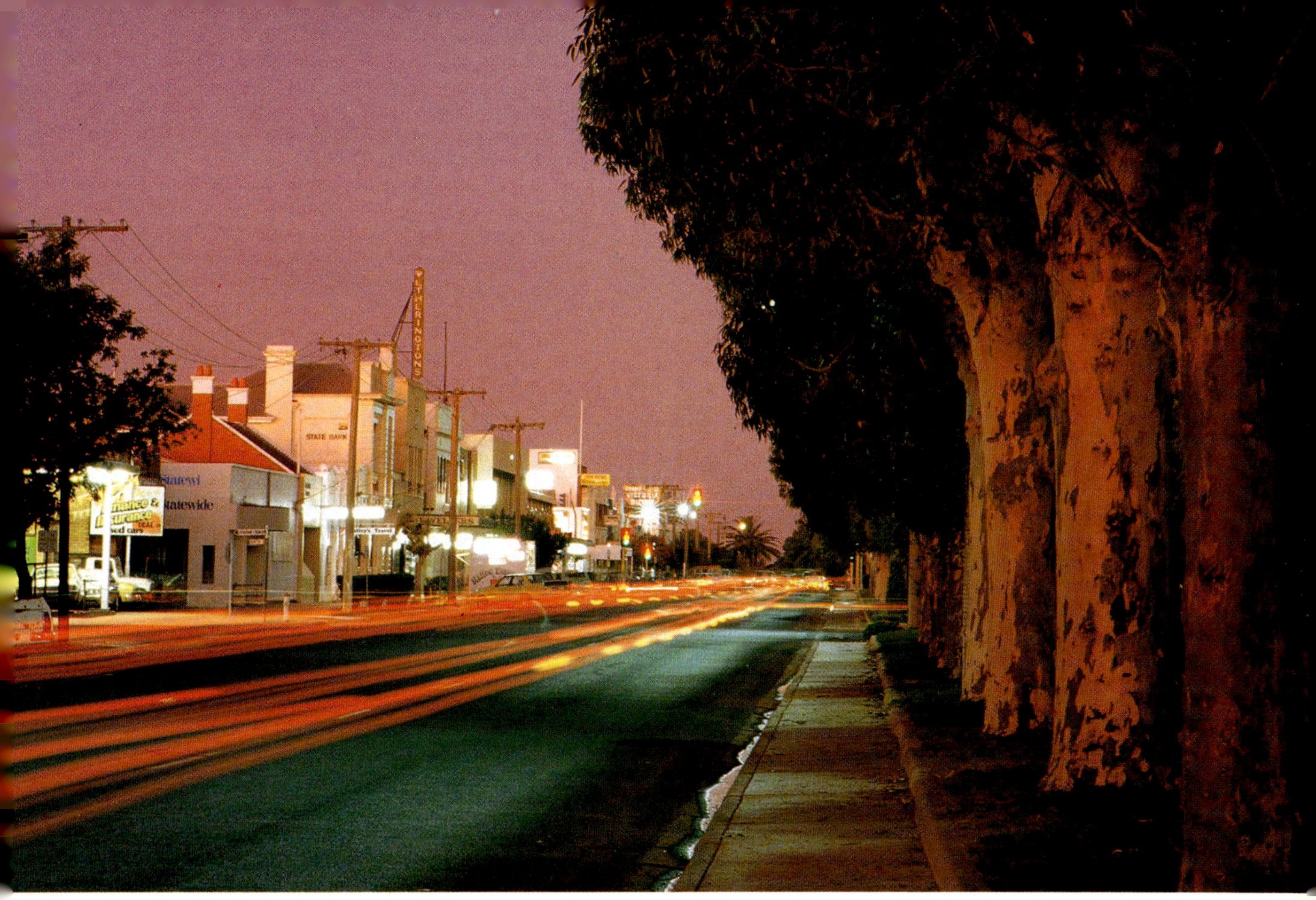
STATE BANK
Statewide

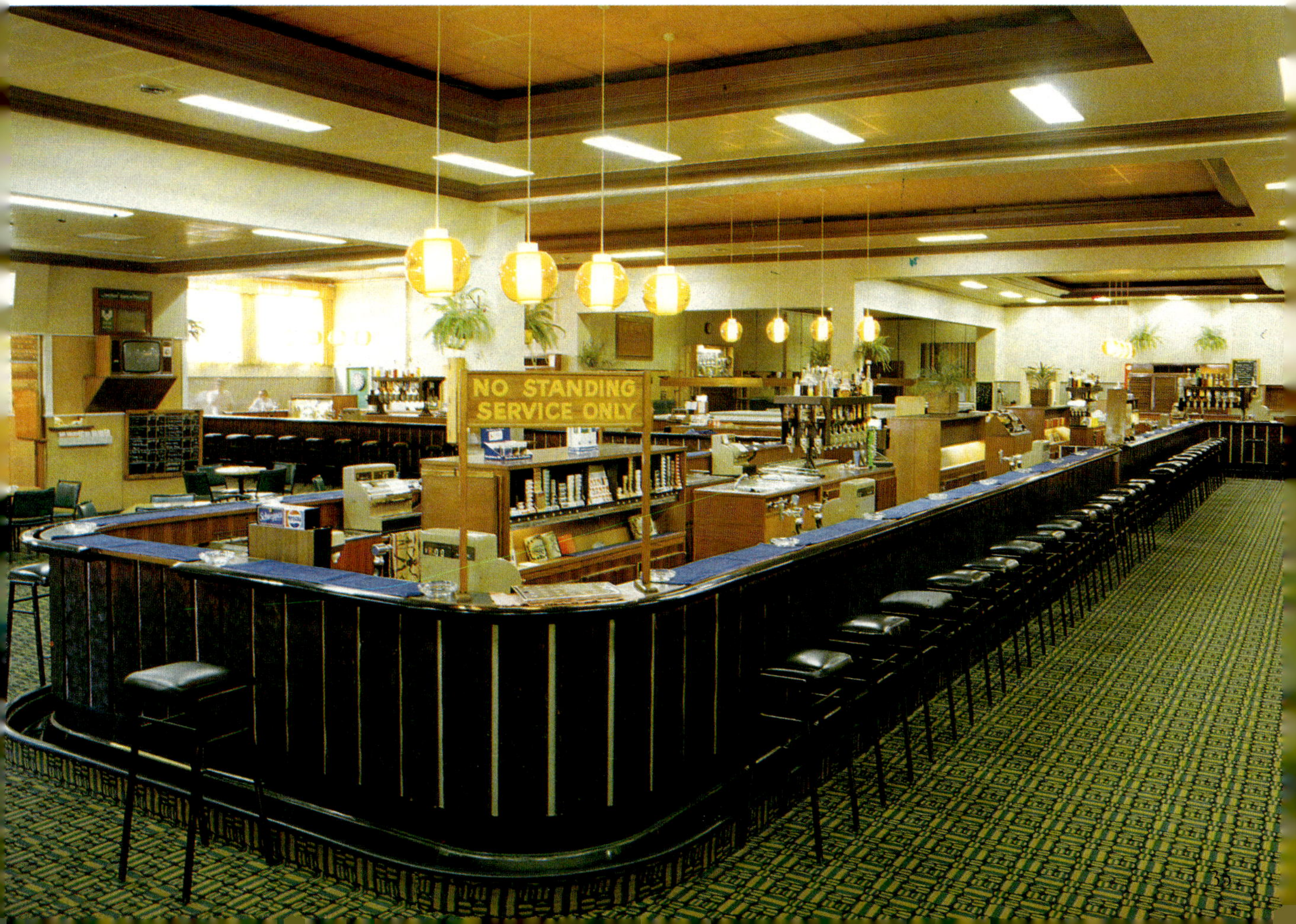
NO STANDING
SERVICE ONLY

Tasmania was discovered in 1642 by Abel Janszoon Tasman, after whom the island state is named, but it was not until 1803 that the first settlement was established. The island's climate and fertile soil allowed agriculture to thrive and soon the colony escaped its penal origins. Even now the economy of Tasmania is basically agricultural, though secondary industry is gaining in importance. Hobart, the capital, (these pages) stands on the estuary of the Derwent River. Above: Mount Wellington, (left) Tasman Bridge and (top) the city from Mount Nelson.

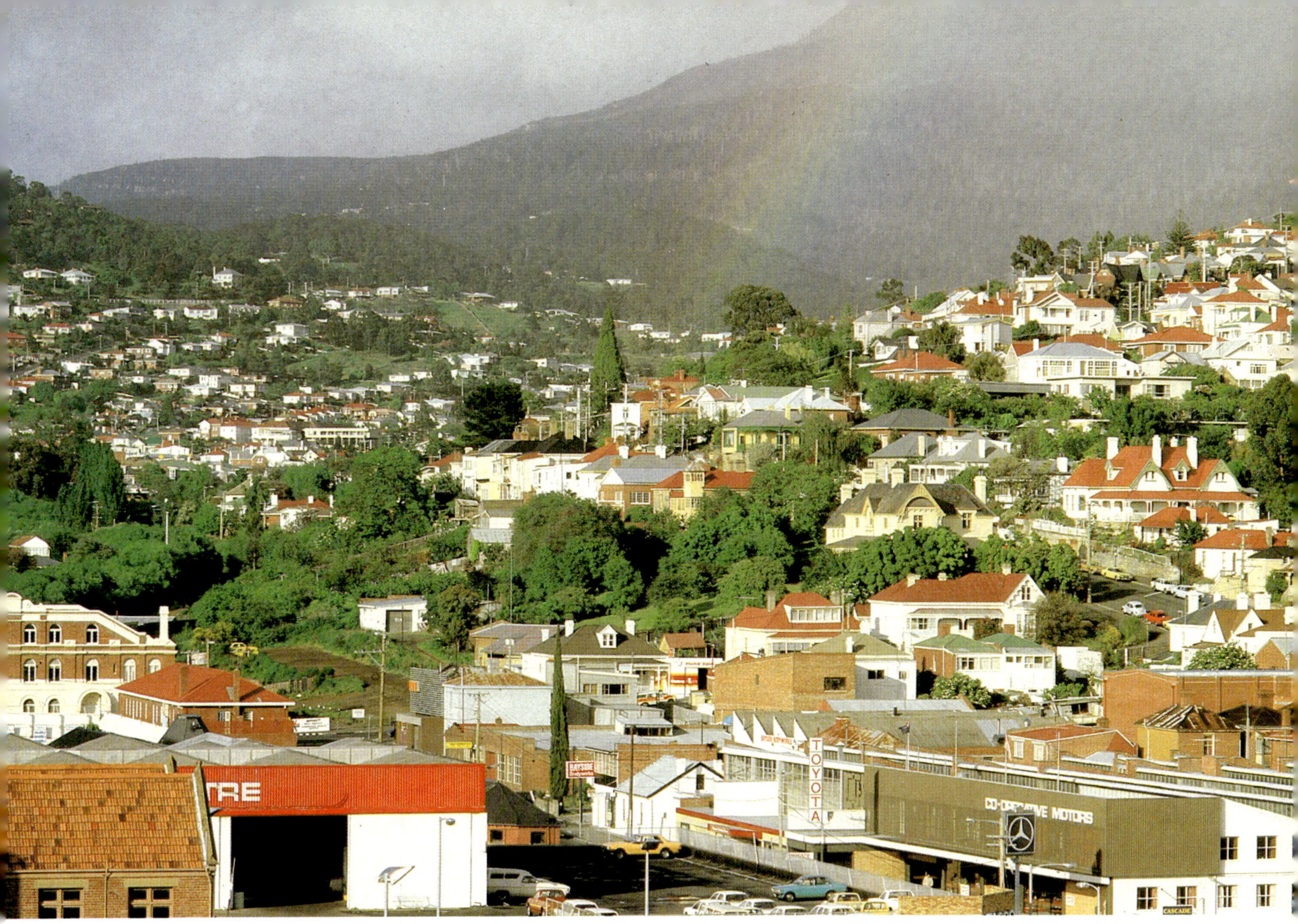
TRE
TOYOTA
CO-OPERATIVE MOTORS

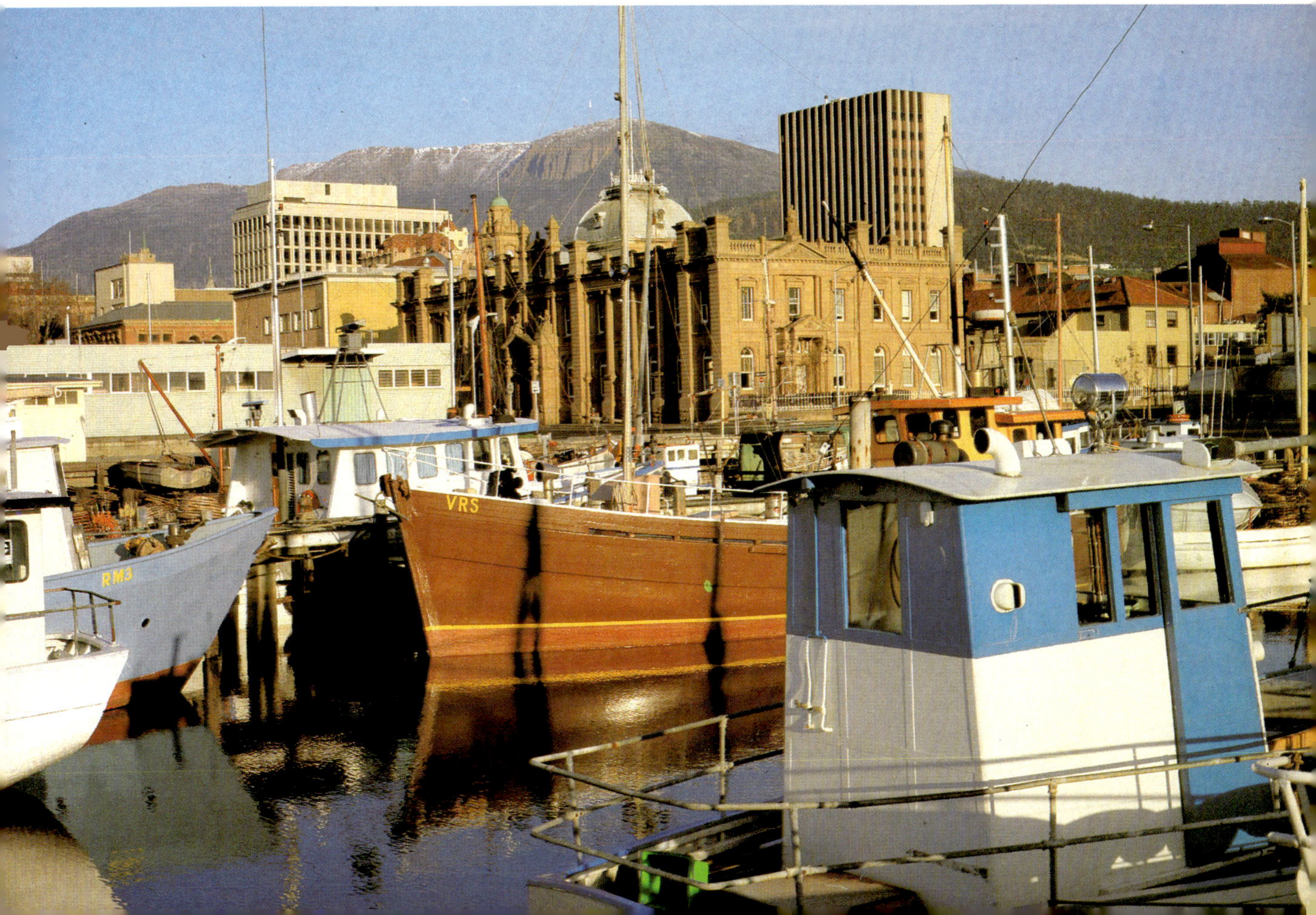
VRS
RM3

Sixty-four kilometres northeast of Hobart stands the Church of Saint John the Baptist (above left), in the small township of Buckland. The church was built in 1846, and its claim to fame lies in its East Window, which dates back to the 14th century, when it was installed in Battle Abbey, England. Above right: the Penny Royal Complex, a major tourist attraction at Launceston (top). Facing page: the spectacular Tasman Arch, a natural rock formation on the east coast of the Tasman Peninsula.

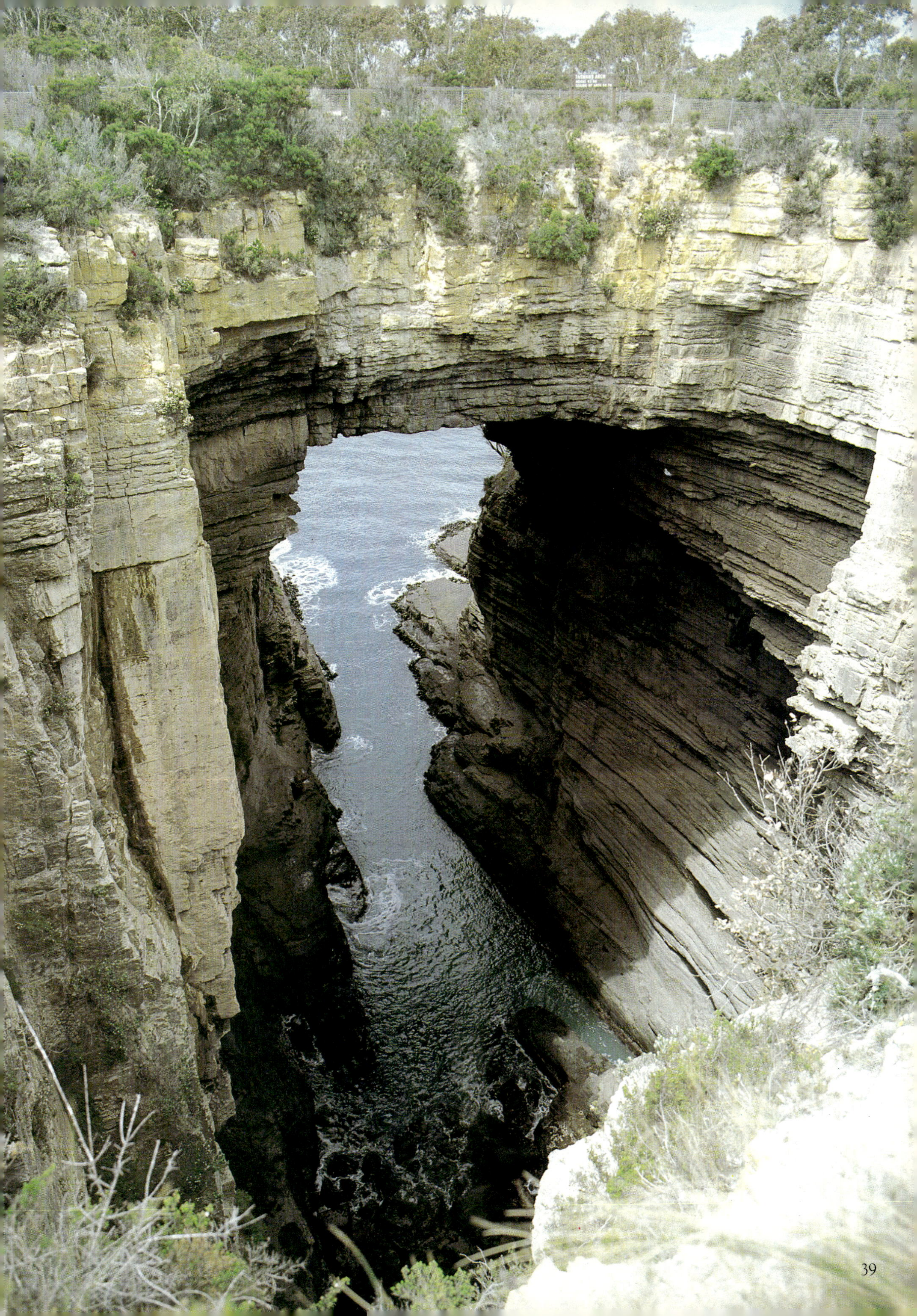

Top: hop fields near Glenora in the Derwent Valley, (left) Russell Falls in Mount Field National Park and (above) the beach at Port Sorrell, near Devonport. Facing page: (top) a catch of lobsters is inspected at Dover, on the D'Entrecasteaux Channel, and (bottom) mountains around the western mining town of Queenstown.

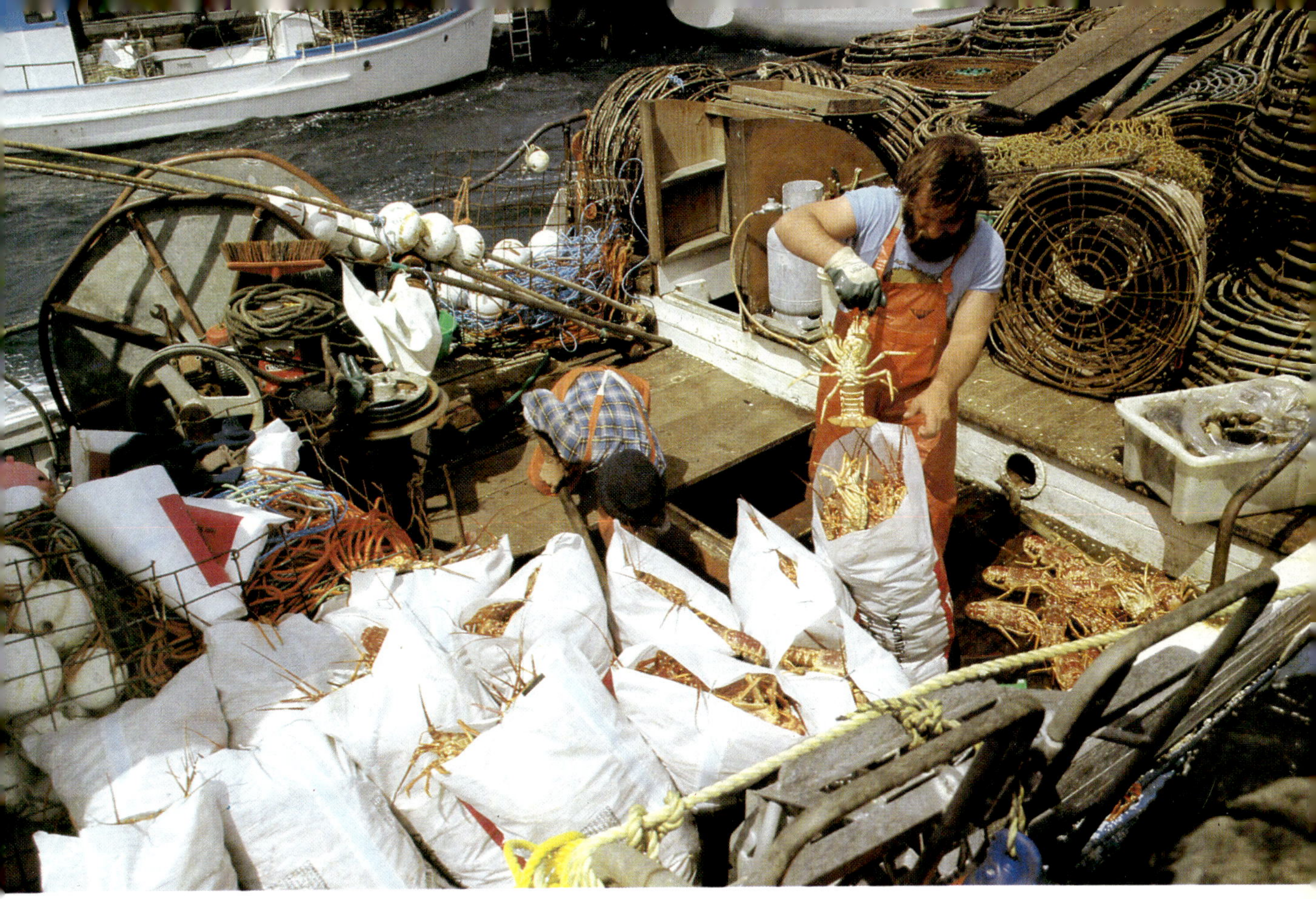

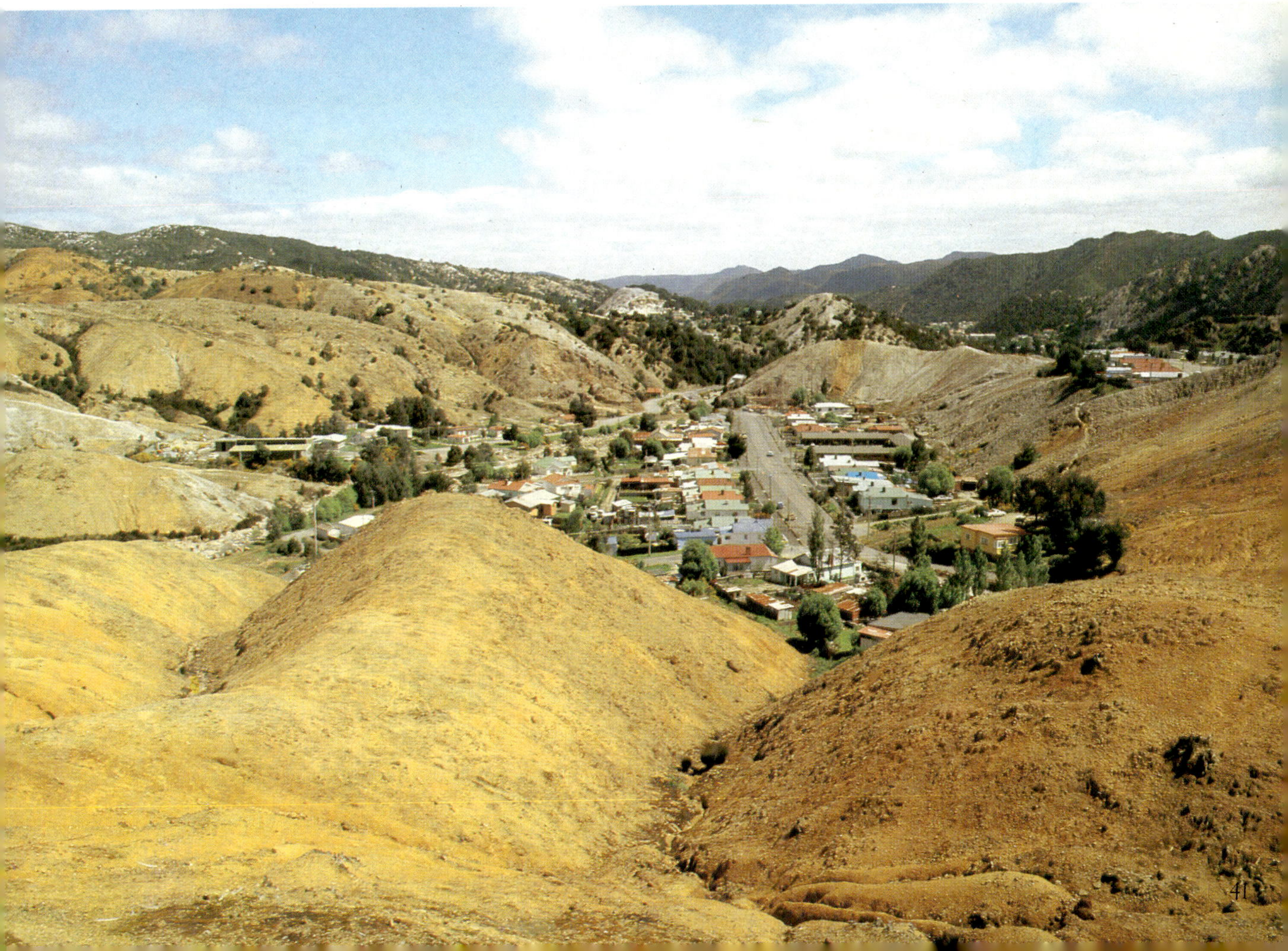

Adelaide, the capital of South Australia, owes its graceful layout to Colonel Light, who planned the city with fine buildings and wide streets such as North Terrace (left). Top: Rundle Mall and (facing page) the spectacular Festival Centre, which graces the capital of the 'Festival State' and is put to good use by its citizens.

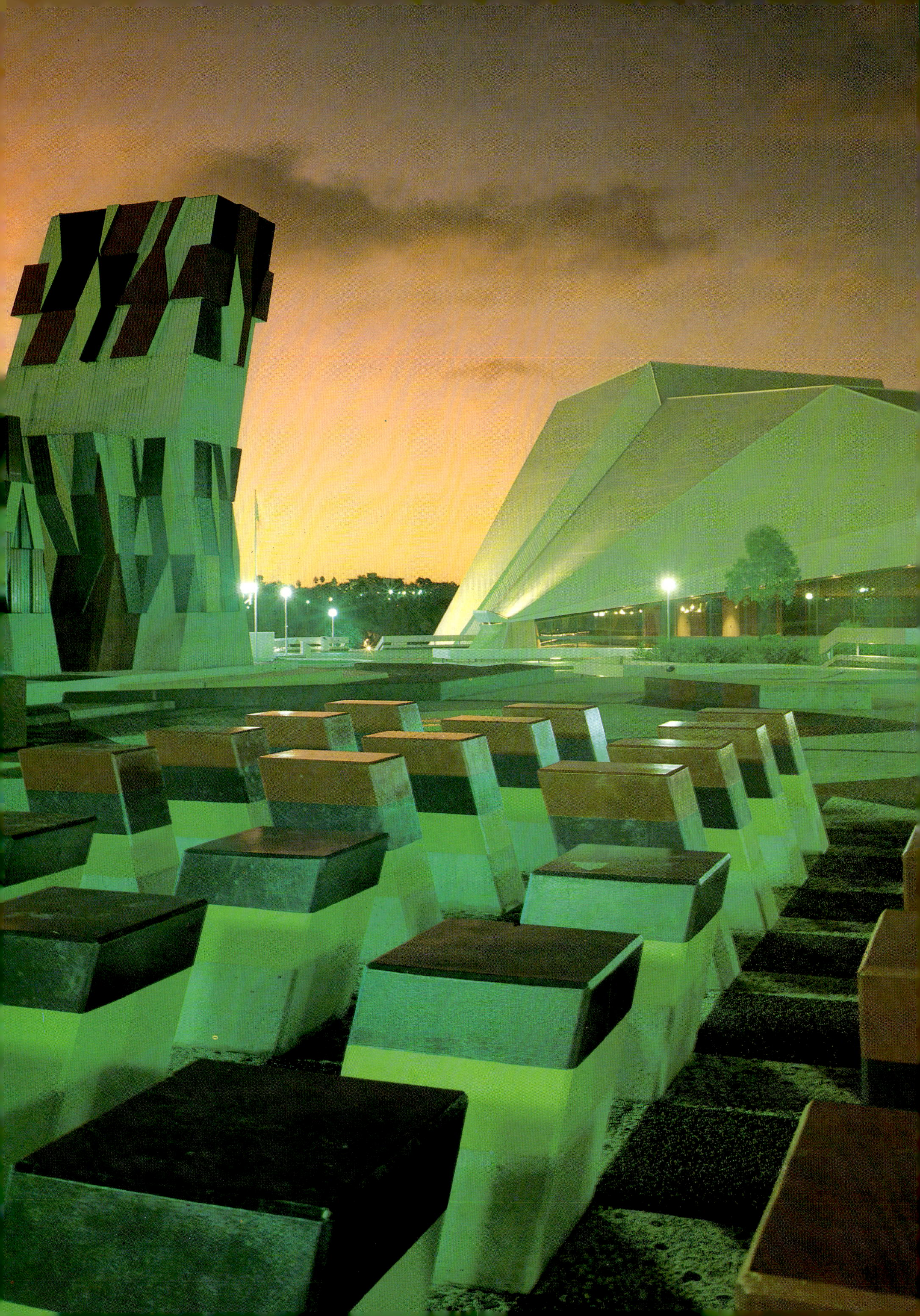

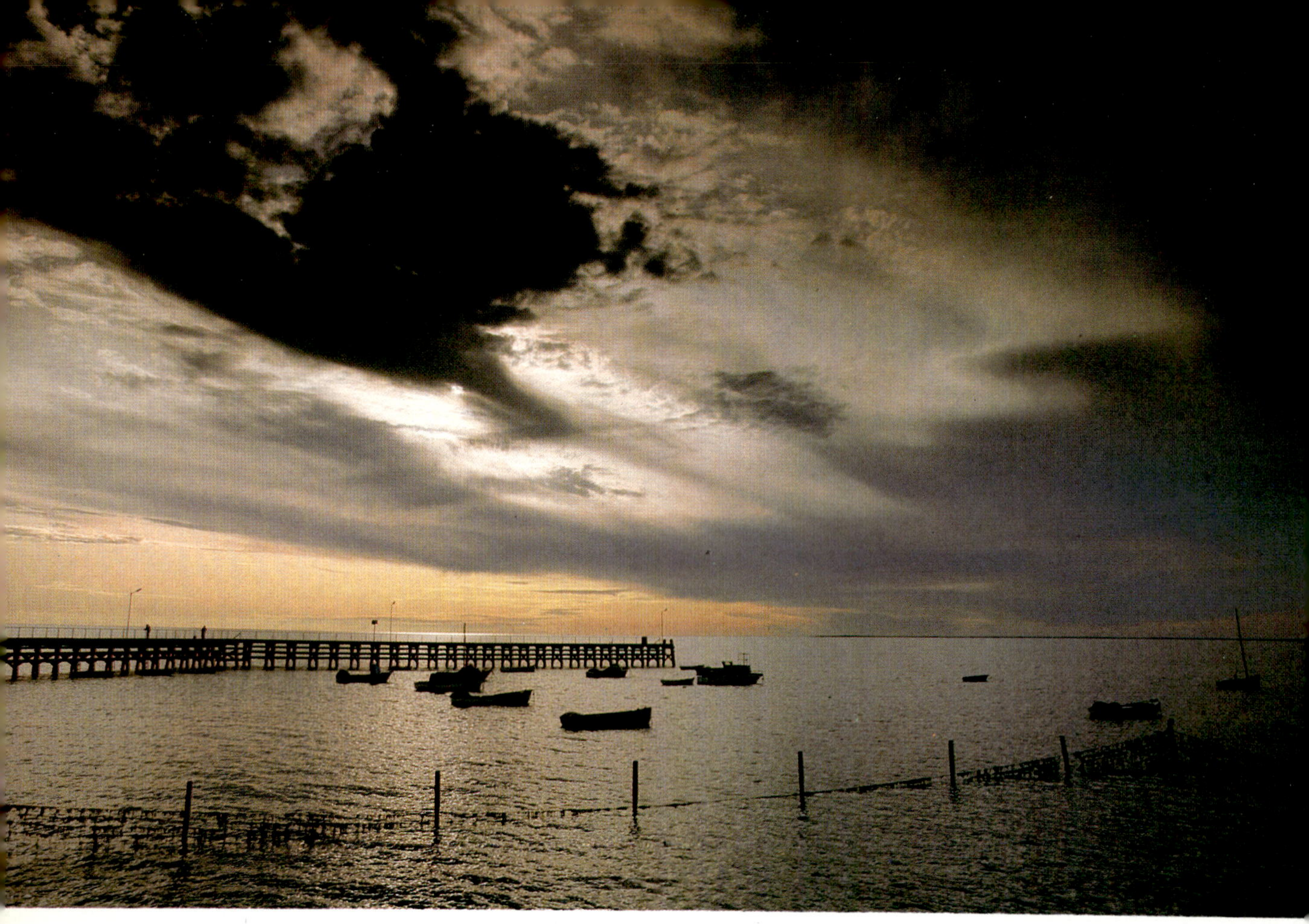

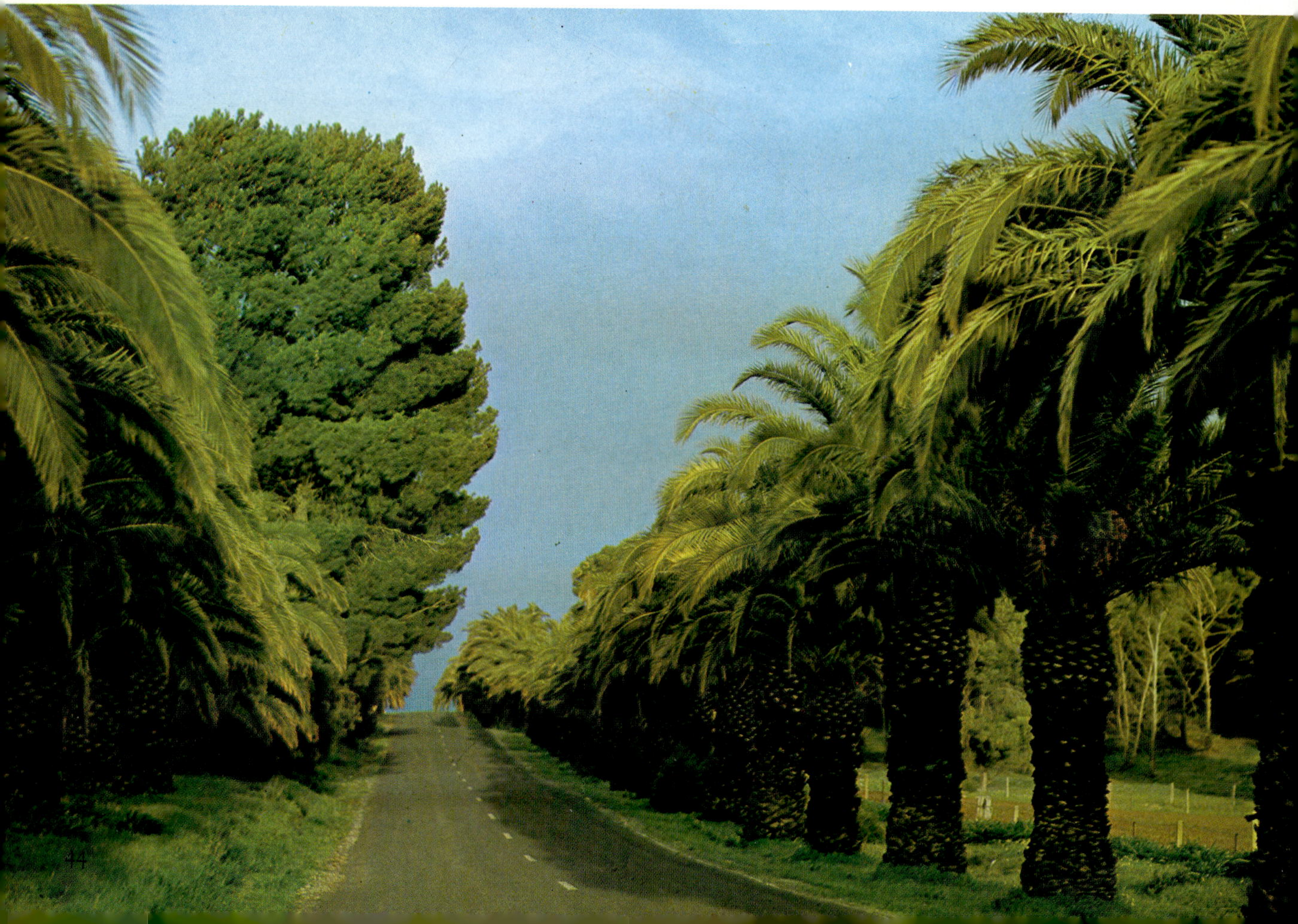

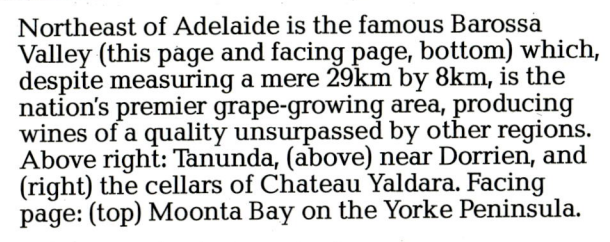

Northeast of Adelaide is the famous Barossa Valley (this page and facing page, bottom) which, despite measuring a mere 29km by 8km, is the nation's premier grape-growing area, producing wines of a quality unsurpassed by other regions. Above right: Tanunda, (above) near Dorrien, and (right) the cellars of Chateau Yaldara. Facing page: (top) Moonta Bay on the Yorke Peninsula.

Above: the Flinders Ranges, near Wilpena. Left: Port Broughton, a small harbour near Kadina (facing page, bottom), which is the main town of the Yorke Peninsula (top). Facing page, top: a view from Hancocks Lookout, near Port Augusta.

47

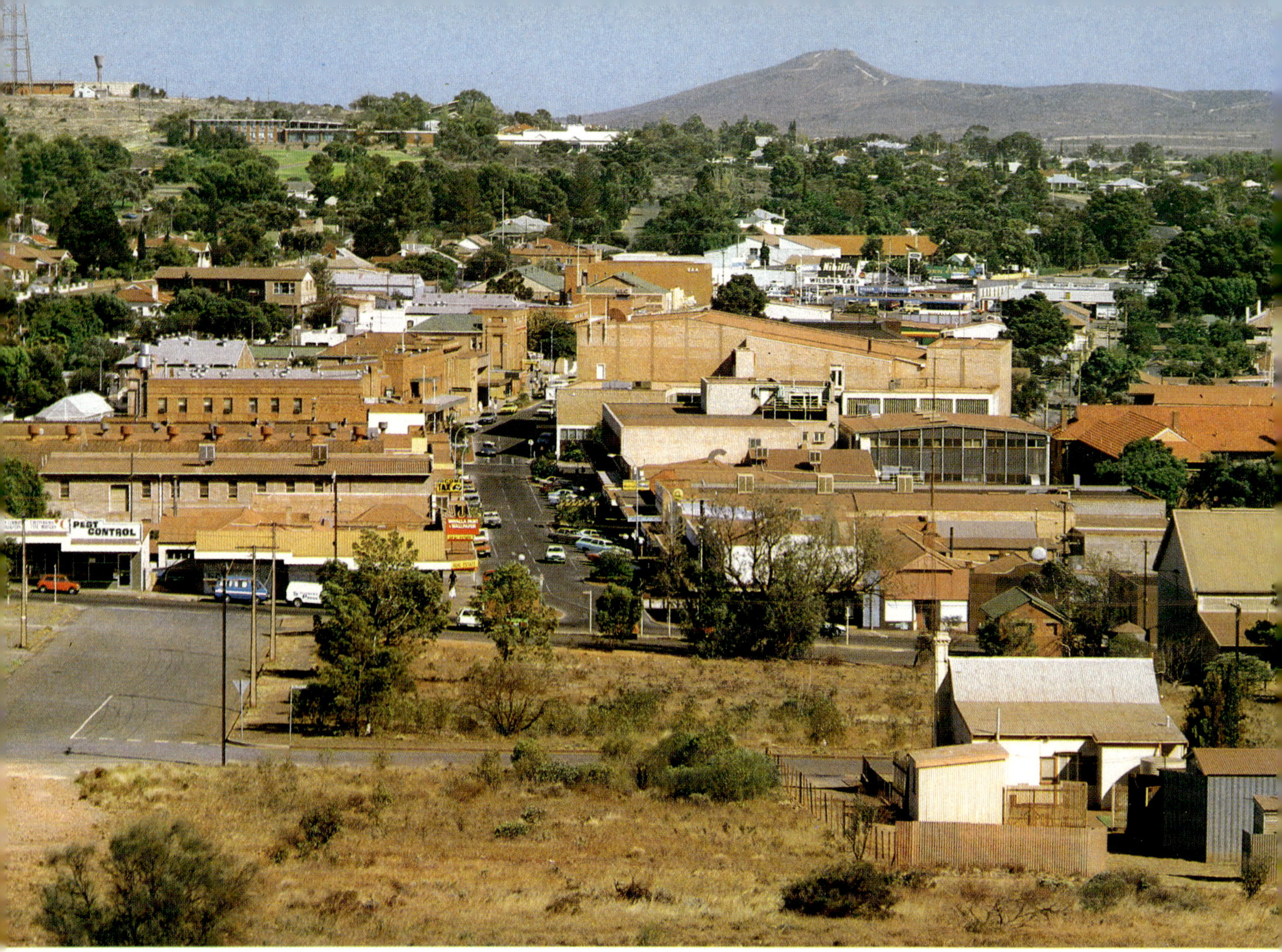
PEST
CONTROL

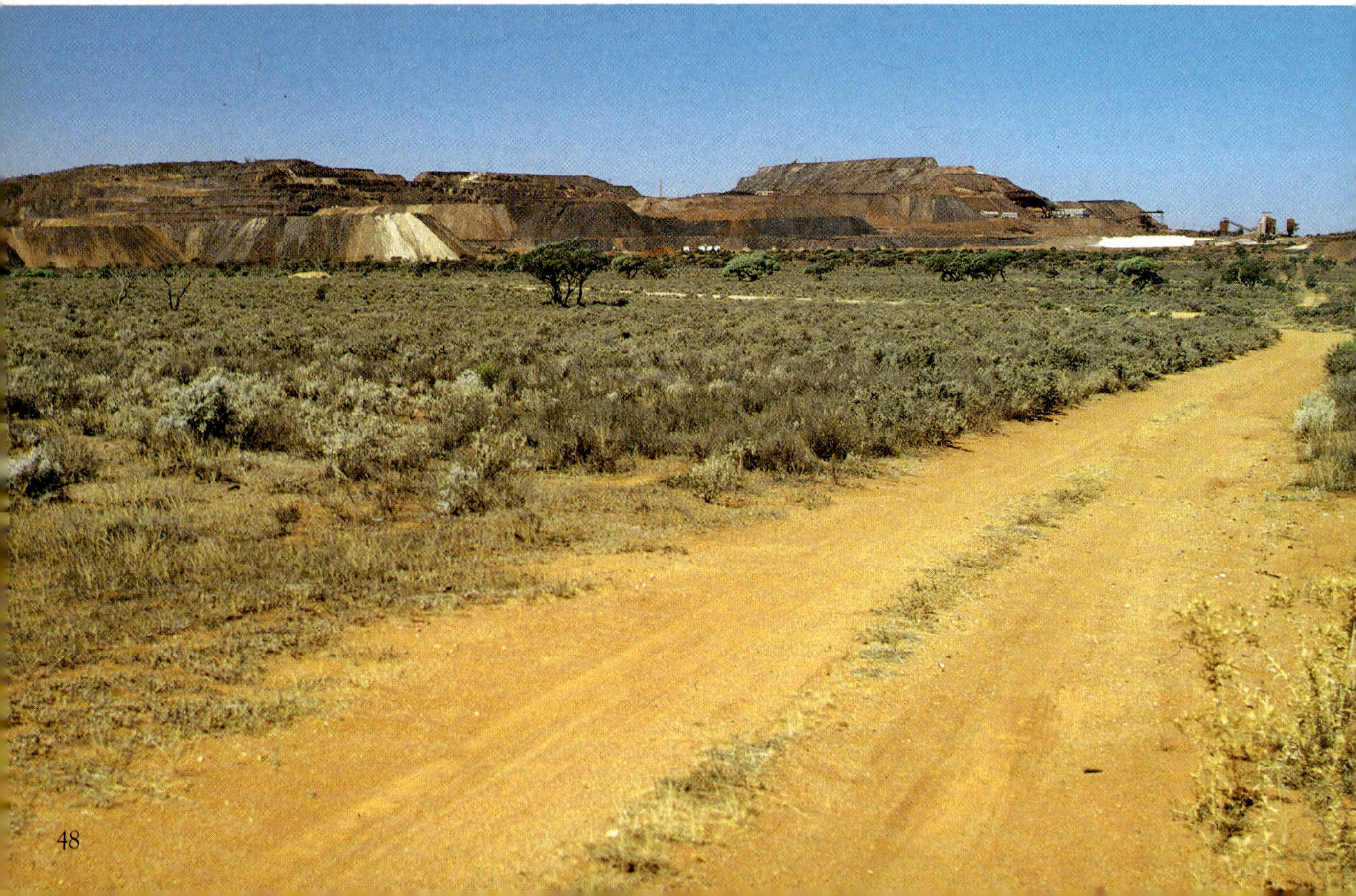

Port Augusta (this page), a prosperous city at the head of Spencer Gulf, forms the supply base for the vast areas of the South Australian Outback. Left: the combined Town Hall and cinema, built in 1887. On the western shore of Spencer Gulf is the larger town of Whyalla (facing page, top), an important industrial city and port which owes its wealth to the iron ore deposits at Iron Knob (facing page, bottom).

The Eyre Peninsula (these pages) is a fascinating area of South Australia, containing a remarkable range of scenery and towns. Above: some typical scrubland around Whyalla. Top: Port Lincoln, which lies at the southernmost tip of the peninsula and, with its Mediterranean climate and fine waters, is rapidly becoming a popular holiday resort. Remaining pictures: Ceduna, in the extreme northwest of the peninsula, showing (left) the Overseas Telecommunications Earth Station and (above left) gypsum awaiting export.

T MART
BUTCHER Health Foods SNACKS-HAIRDRESSER EmJay SHOES
Butcher
Snacks
HAIR STYLIST
CHEM
TACKLE-BAIT
Adela

Western Australia has some of the most spectacular and majestic scenery in the country, including (top) the beautiful Porongorup Range, north of Albany, with some of its unusual flora (above), and (left) the bridge in Yallingup National Park. Facing page: (bottom) the extraordinary Wave Rock near Hyden and (top) the coast near Wyadup.

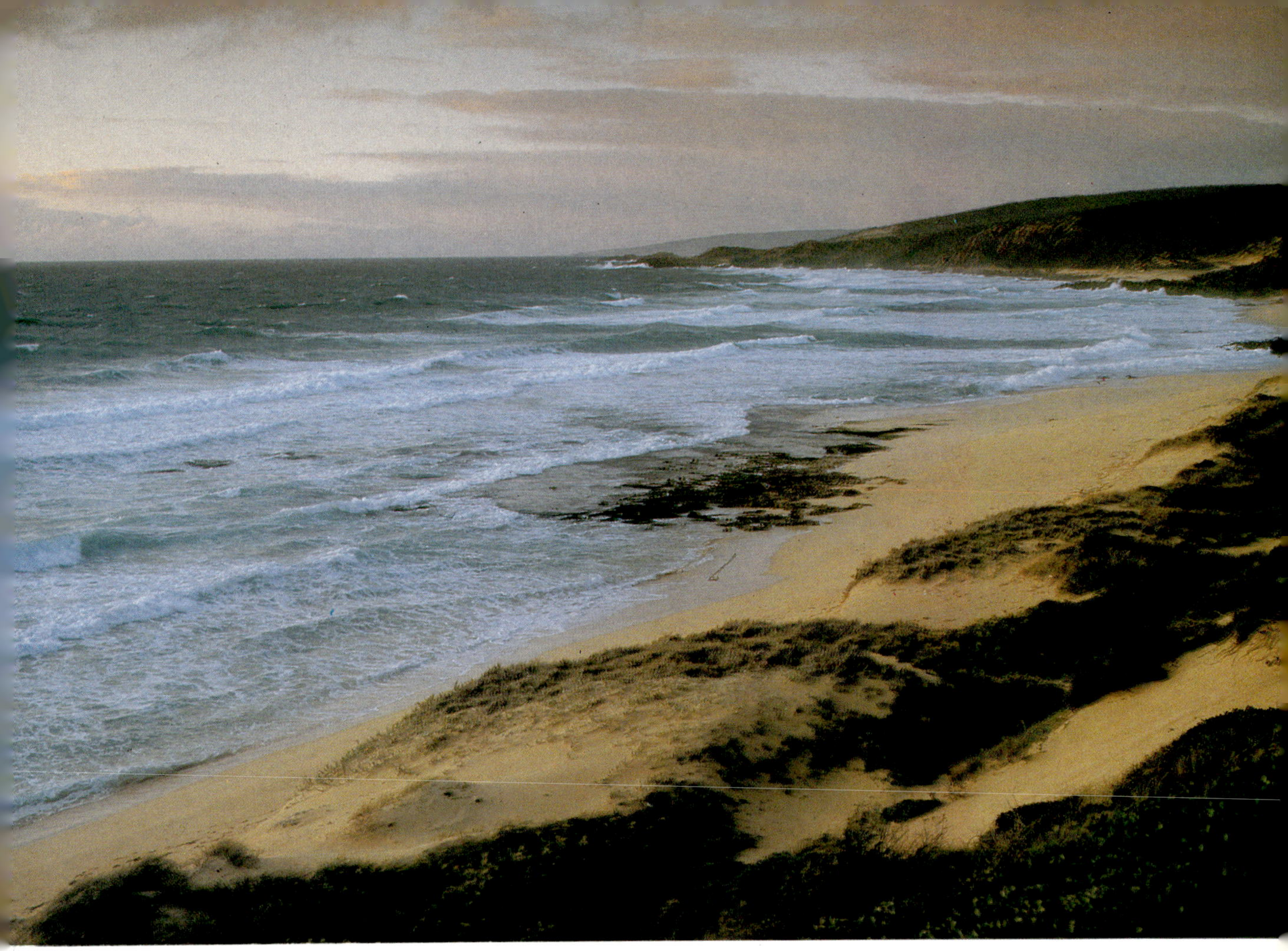

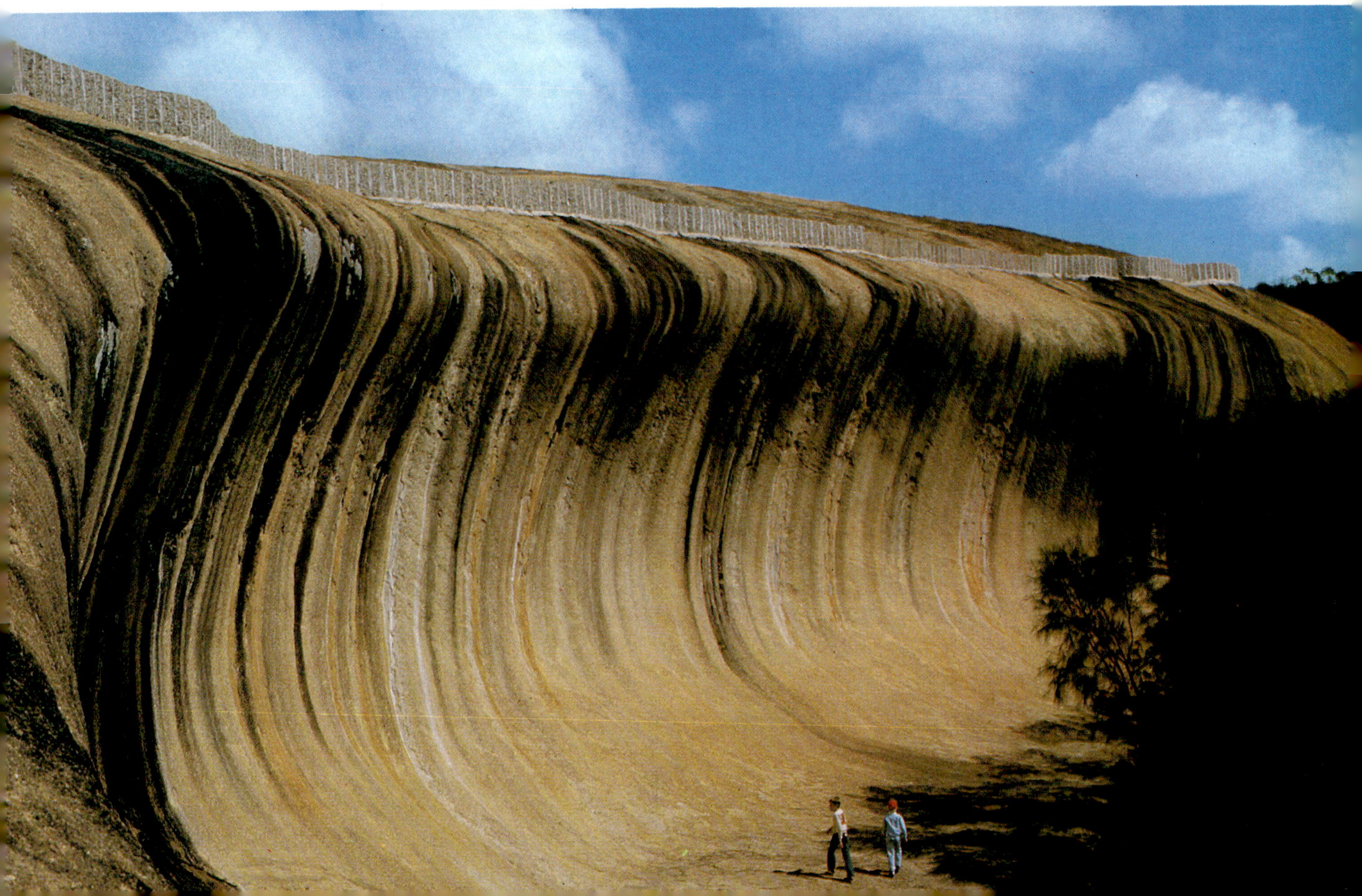

The lovely city of Perth is the capital of Western Australia and the sunshine capital of the nation, enjoying an average of 7.8 hours of brilliant sun a day. The city's buildings display a variety of architectural styles, as seen in Barrack Street (left), Murray Street (above), William Street (below) and London Court (top left). Facing page: (bottom) the Cathedral and (top) the gardens around the Parliament Buildings.

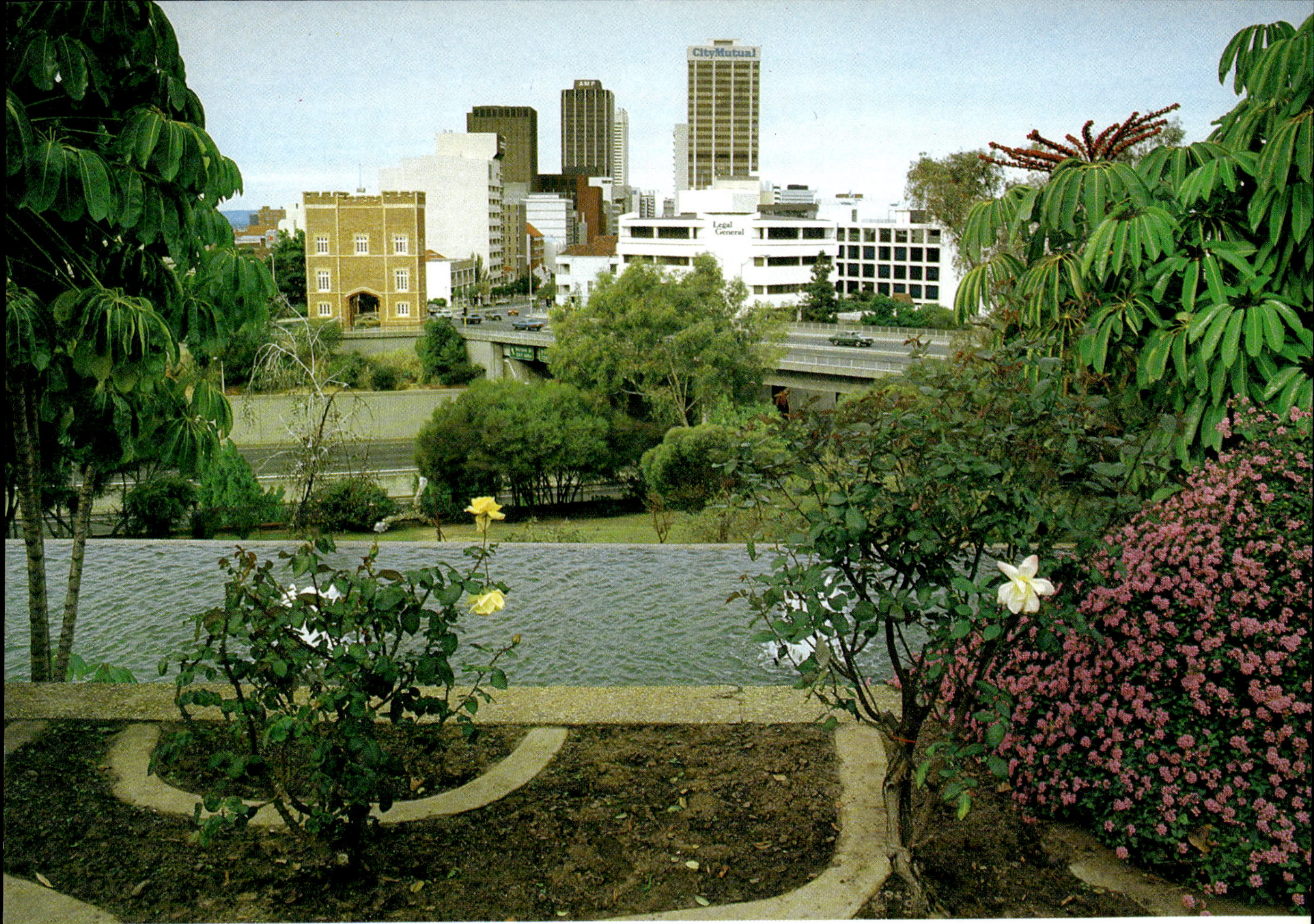
CityMutual

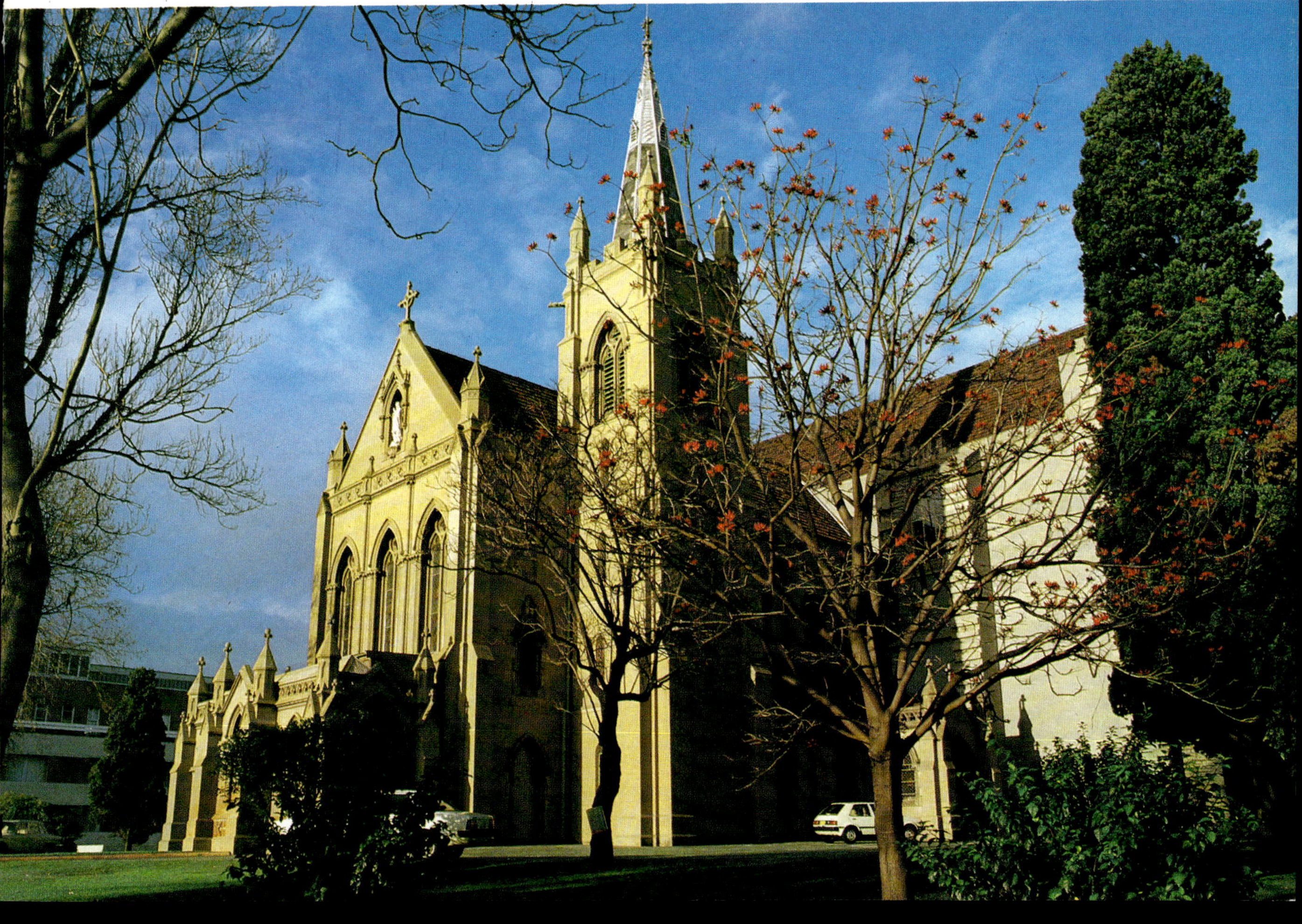

Above: a shady waterhole within the Hamersley Range National Park. Top: bands of coloured sandstone at Kalbarri National Park. Left: a giant termite mound in the Hamersley Range. Facing page: the strange 'Pinnacles' in Nambung National Park.

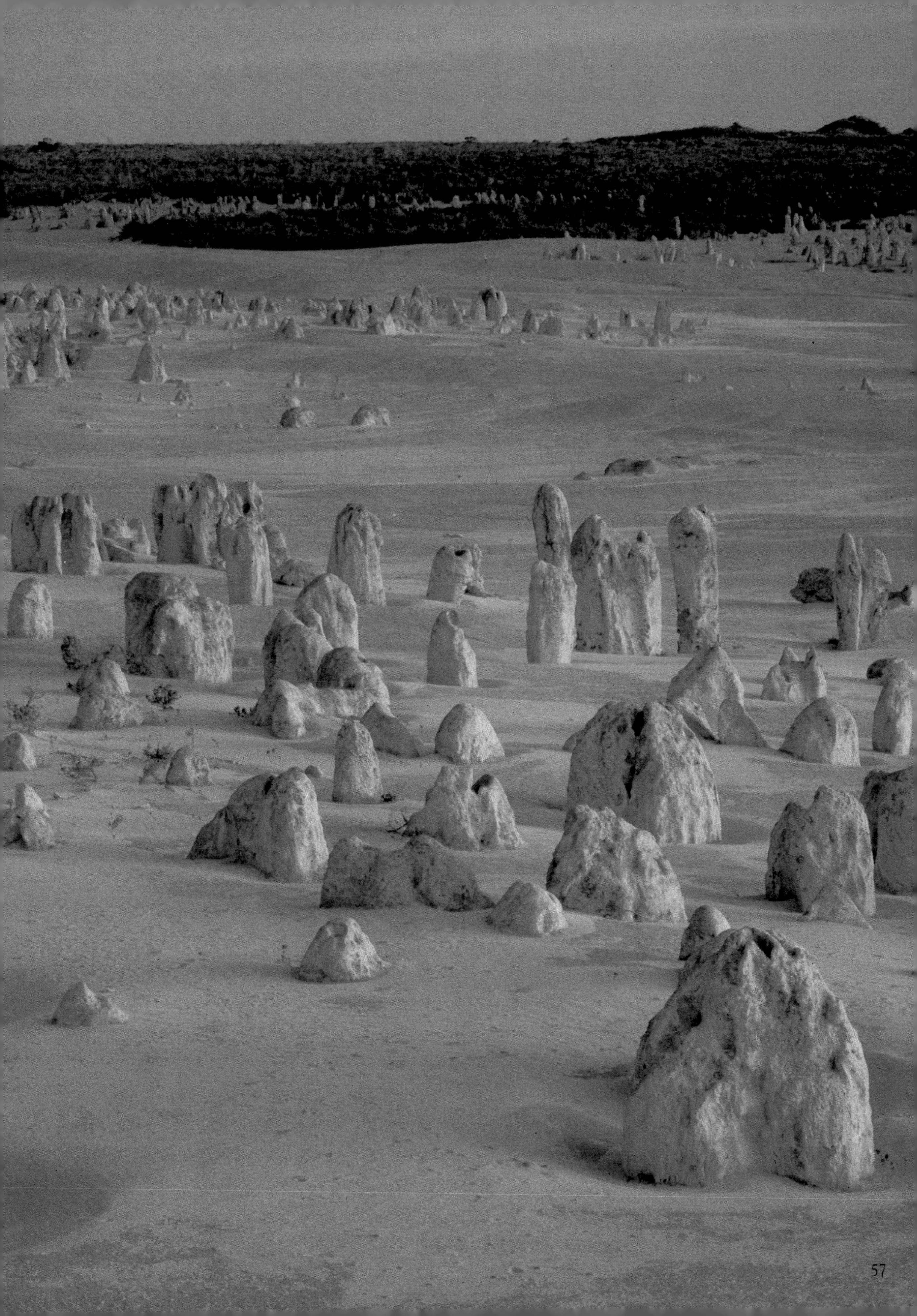

Darwin (these pages) is the major city in the Northern Territory. For many years the city's development was hampered by isolation, but the Stuart Highway and the mineral wealth of the territory injected life into the city. Since Cyclone Tracy struck in 1974, Darwin has been rebuilt in a fine, new style. Bottom right and facing page, top: Smith Street. Right: Christchurch Cathedral, which was completed in 1977 at a cost of $800,000. Facing page, bottom: the Law Courts. Above: the luxurious, modern casino which overlooks the Timor Sea at Mindil Beach.

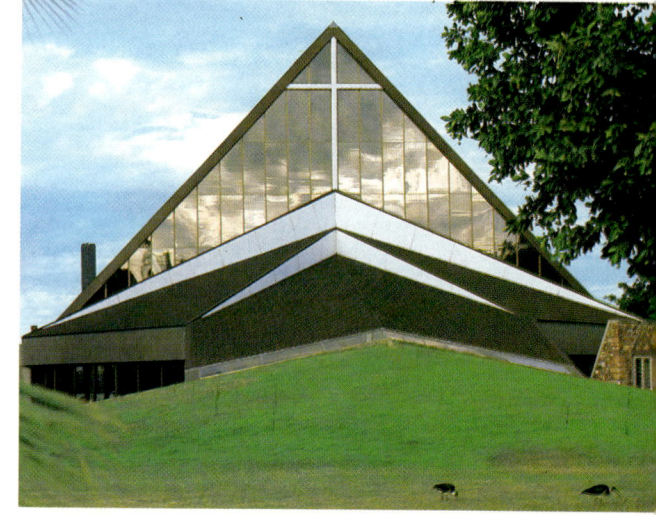

59

Above: the prestigious Civic Centre at Tennant Creek. Alice Springs (remaining pictures) stands at the very heart of the 'Red Centre'. The town had its origins with the Old Telegraph Station (facing page, top) over a century ago. Below: the Control Station of the Royal Flying Doctor Service. Right: the John Flynn Memorial Church; Flynn was a missionary who founded the flying doctor service. Bottom right: the Riverside Hotel. Facing page, bottom: Todd Plaza.

TELEGRAPH
OFFICE

SPORTS LOTTO
BOOK SHOP
LARGE RANGE QUALITY BOOKS & AUSTRALIANA
BOOK SHOP
TODD

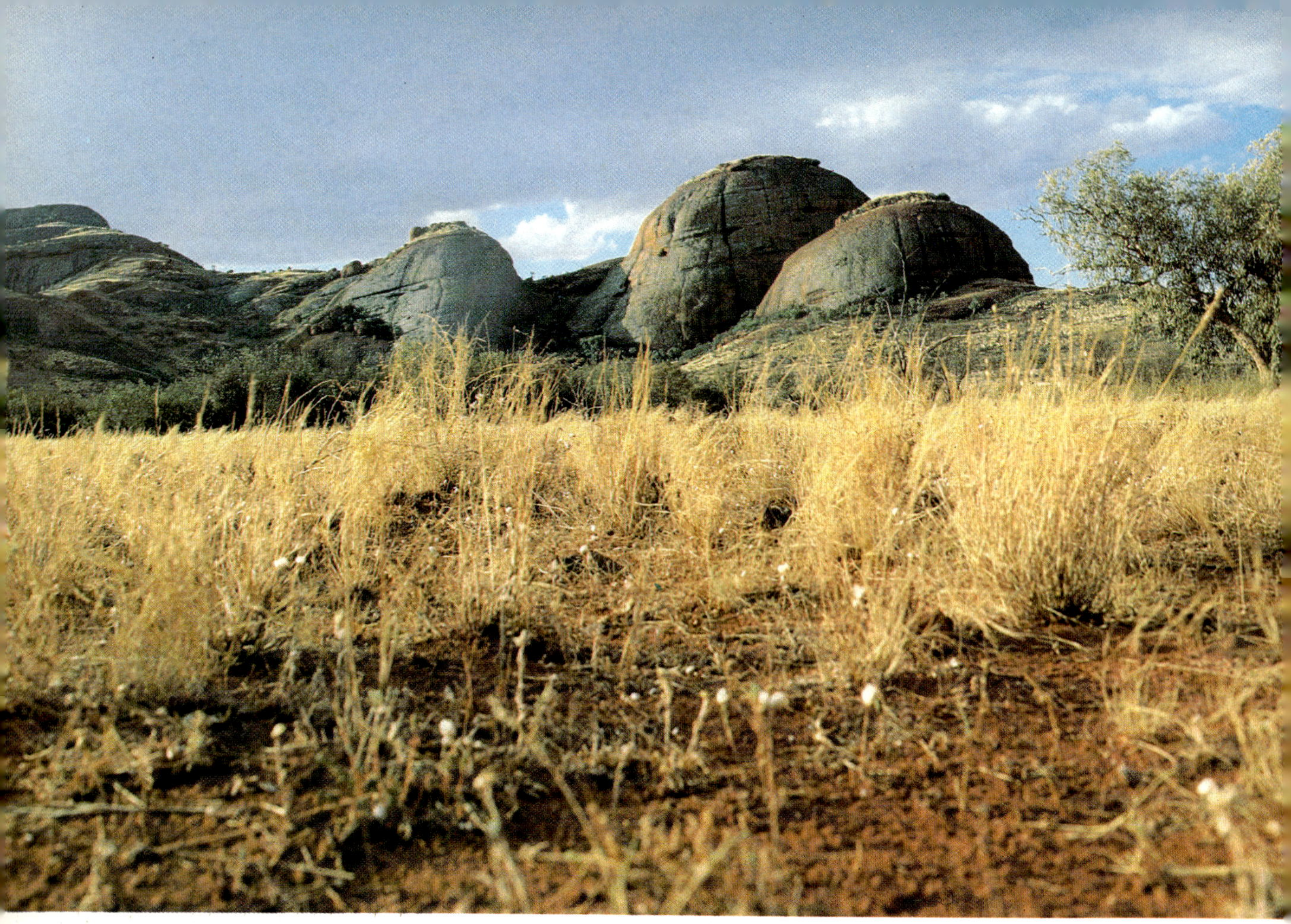
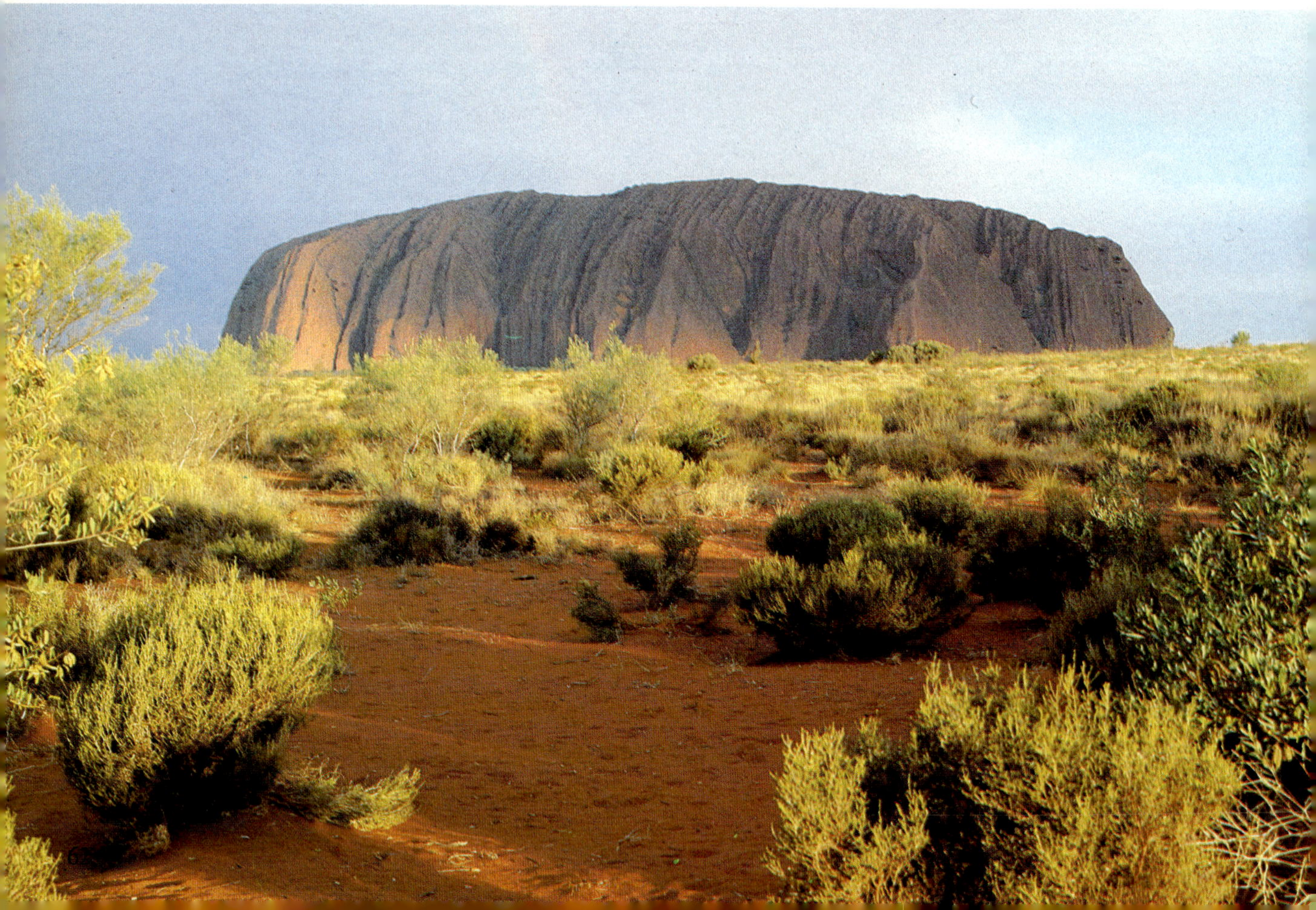

Bottom: Ormiston National Park, where a stream cuts through the Macdonell Ranges to form a gorge. Right: the Palm Valley Fauna and Flora Reserve. The palms were found by the explorer Ernest Giles in 1872. Facing page: (top) the Olgas and (bottom) the famous Ayers Rock. Overleaf: Standley Chasm, in the West Macdonnell Ranges.